LIFE IS A BEACH

A tale of subculture in the early 80's

Dave Andrews

Copyright © 2025 Dave Andrews

All rights reserved

The characters and events portrayed in this book are fictitious. Any similarity to real persons, living or dead, is coincidental and not intended by the author.

No part of this book may be reproduced, or stored in a retrieval system, or transmitted in any form or by any means, electronic, mechanical, photocopying, recording, or otherwise, without express written permission of the publisher.

ISBN: 9798311825504

I dedicate this book to my beach buddy Jerry, without whom my life would have been far less colourful. This trip most certainly happened through Jerry's sense of fun and adventure. Forty years on I'm still proud to call him my friend. Cheers Jerry, bigtime, you know it.

LIFE IS A BEACH

A Tale Of Subculture In The Early Eighties.

An unlikely group of friends take to the road in a classic camper. Destination the South of France, to become beach doughnut sellers. Based on a true story.

It's the summer of 83. A summer I know I will always remember, one that's turned my life around.

I'm sitting here on an empty beach looking eastwards out across the Mediterranean away from the setting sun behind me. The sea is a calm silvery blue with dark purple razor-sharp horizon. There's barely a wave lapping on the shore. It's windless and still. Large areas of sea are glassy smooth, others have a silky finish.

I'm alone, taking a bit of time out, a moment to myself with a large plastic bottle of beer straight from the chest freezer.

I never got round to changing, so still in a self-imposed work uniform. White shorts, white shirt, and a straw hat. My hat is next to me on my small scrap of woven beach mat, the sun has gone, no need for it now.

Burying my bare feet through the dry warm top sand to the cooler layer below. I'm thinking… 'Life is good'.

Stars are appearing on the far horizon as if turning on one at a time. Reassuring distant sounds of music travel effortlessly through the still night air. Campsite clubs and town bars competing for holiday makers… chasing the franc. Not for me this evening. I'm good here, there is a time for these things and now isn't it.

To have found this very spot is quite unreal. I simply can't imagine it working out better. Behind me, a few hundred yards down, is the Café on a hill, run by our now good friends and employers, the Gypsies. Behind that is where we live, a guarded car park by day and home by night.

To my right, South, is darkness, until lit up in the far distance, the tourist development of the Cap

D'Agde.

North, to my left, the land of milk and honey. Left is where it's at. Stretching several miles is an uninterrupted golden sandy beach. The top edge is lined continuously with campsites catering for different individual nationalities.

For the first mile most of the European nations are covered, then bingo! The golden goose… The English beach. Deeper and as long as all the others combined. Half a mile of bi-weekly rotating two-week holiday makers. Hotel campers. Here for the sun, sea, sand and sex… and unbeknown to them 'the doughnuts!'. That's where we come in.

Two months ago I had a steady job in a green part of South East London working as a groundsman. It was okay, not really what I wanted to do but it paid money and wasn't too demanding. Mostly in summer I'd be cutting grass with a tractor and gang mowers and spending hours every day rolling cricket strips.

I'd been there for about a year and a half and there was no sign of anything on the horizon, that is until Jerry and I took a trip to Canterbury one weekend one week in early June in his camper, to a student party some friends of ours were having.

Their plan, we discovered, was to head off to France directly after their exams to sell doughnuts and ice creams on the beach. This idea sounded good to us, and with Jerry having a camper van they were more than pleased for us to tag along. The four of them had pre-arranged jobs and a time and location to head for. Just over a week away.

My employers were surprised when I handed in my notice on Monday morning. They protested, 'You must be mad!' and 'What are you thinking?' 'You could have had a career here.' But my mind was made up. This was happening, and it was going to be fun.

One short week later we were meeting up to pack our gear in the van. One of the Canterbury four, Bill, is a good friend of ours. The others we just met last week at the party. Jerry has booked the ferry tickets, although he has only booked for two adults, so it will be a case of heads down for tickets then back up for passports. He does beer runs to Calais on a regular basis and says they'll never notice. They didn't.

After an evening crossing and smooth journey down through the night we arrive in darkness in the early hours. Everyone trying to make the best of available space, we decide to sleep it out in the camper until morning. When dawn arrives, and we clamber out to stretch, we are dismayed by the beach which was absolutely nothing like we had pictured. A narrow stretch of sand with a deep band of black dried seaweed swarming with tiny flies leading to a still expanse of water. This can't be it. It wasn't.

The town of Marseillan Ville where we had found ourselves lies on the Basin Du Thau, an expanse of inland salt water separated from the sea. Where we were actually headed was Marseillan Plage, a new town and tourist development on the nearby Mediterranean coast.

Not keen to get straight back in the van, the Canterbury 4 wanted to discover the old town of Marseillan Ville and maybe get some breakfast. Jerry and I decide to go on a recce… on a quest to find the real beach and come back for them in a couple of hours.

Driving through the busy streets of Marseillan Plage is an experience. Like driving through a blizzard… of people. Except you have to wait for each one to get out of the way. Perhaps more like the parting of the Red Sea. We drive an endless road thick with humanity, café terraces, campsites, restaurants and shops line each side so there's not a chance of anywhere to stop or any view of the sea.

Eventually, further along the road, the crowds

start to dissipate, but there is still no parking until right at the very end. A hand-painted sign reads 'Parking Gardé'. "Guarded Parking," I translate. Jerry glares at me, even he understands that. "Well, we might as well, what else are we going to do?" I say.

The sign directs us along a small track running along the far edge of town, in what we hope to be the direction of the beach, until we arrive at the car park. We pay our money to the man at the gate, who we now know to be Alain, and that's where it started. We were not to know this would be our ultimate destination and serve all our needs.

Still with no view of the sea but with the sand dunes a sense it was very close, we parked the van and walk towards the beach. Ahh. That's more like it. Unbelievable… unforgettable, a deep blue turquoise sea rumbling in frothy white waves big enough to push you about, but not fully bowl you over.

Our feet sink into the hot sand for the first time, a feeling we would get to know so well. A quick hop back to the camper to change and grab a towel and we dive right in. Heaven. This was it, why we'd come. I mostly remember the Mediterranean as being a bit waveless, so this was an extra welcome surprise, repeatedly wading out to get crashed back in by the next big tumbler.'

After an hour or so in the surf we let ourselves sun dry, then head up a steep wooden staircase to the café. Our first meeting with the Gypsies. We got into conversation with Felix the head man and sat with him at his table. He told us of how the car park used to be a beautiful campsite with regular visitors coming every year and about how the council had not renewed their licence, so they have had to re purpose the land as a car park.

Looking down on the car park I could see a small two roomed house on one floor with a terracotta roof and concrete patio slab in front. And in front of that, a large area of sand and grass not suitable for parking cars.

I asked if it would be okay for us to camp there just for tonight until we find our employers and our proper place to stay. He ponders this in his usual fashion while twisting his long grey moustache He says that's okay but if the police should come around and spot us, we may have to move on, but this is very unlikely.

Time to collect the others and bring them back here, involving two journeys through the sea of tourists. We find them sitting in the main square in Marsellian Ville where we had left them. Apart from them, it's deserted. They are not looking so happy.

'Hey guys, you have a good morning?'

'Not really, town was closed.'

'What, all of it?'

'Yep, the whole bloody town. Where are all the people?'

Jerry jokes, 'I think we found them.

Arriving back at Marsellian Plage they are as happy and amazed as we were. Parking back in the same spot they get their first glimpse of the actual sea. After another good long swim, we catch a sight of what we've come to do. A beach seller. A bedraggled figure struggling through the deep hot sand with regular desperate pleas of what sounded like Ben-yay. This turned out to be 'beignet', The French translation for doughnut.

To be honest, it didn't look great. I think we all had our moment of doubt. It turned out to be a lesson on how not to do it. We were to take this same basic premise of walking the beach and calling out our wares but make it our own.

It didn't start off so easily, the following day, after a morning swim in the sea, we packed down our makeshift camp and after bidding farewell and settling up with the gypsies head off to rendezvous with our future employers to find our permanent camp.

We find the meeting spot, a sandy gravel car park at the opposite edge of town but are a bit early and there is no one there to meet us. There are some lost souls with rucksacks standing and sitting around in the shade of a line of trees running down the centre of the car park. As time passes, they grow in number until there are maybe 14 or 15.

Rolling into the car park throwing up fine sandy dust comes a white van with the name 'Gerard' proudly displayed on its side. It pulls up under the trees the driver opens the back doors, and the gathered backpackers climb in. Again, not quite as we'd imagined it.

We were the only ones with our own transport and were instructed to follow the van as it tore along straight flat roads in land several miles. Then a right turn along a gravel road for another mile struggling to keep up in the swirling dust wake of the van in front. Sometimes clear, and sometimes like driving through fog.

We arrive at a run-down farm, that might have been beautiful if not for the piles of old scrap and plastic that lay everywhere. The backpackers clamber out hot and shaken by the drive.

They, and we are directed to a small field behind the farm, a desolate Patch of land dedicated as the workers campsite. Mostly dry bare earth with occasional patches of sharp spiny undergrowth. It was desperate, not somewhere you'd choose to go on holiday, especially as we had fresh in our minds the location of our previous night.

Hmm. What to do? After a discussion with Gerrard himself it's agreed if we can find our own place to camp, we can meet them at a designated spot, and they will take us to work. It turns out this is quite common. The Canterbury four choose to stick with us, had we not been there this would have been their lot.

Our first shift the following morning, pick up at 10:00 AM from the same car park as this morning. We could have avoided that whole drive had we known. It's a really hot day and we are relieved to be headed back to the coast while the others we leave behind struggle to put their tents up in the full glare of the late morning sun.

Where to? We know we have to find somewhere to camp but at this moment the sea is a greater priority, and the closest we know we can park to it is back in the gypsy car park, so we head there. Alain takes our money; this is our third time and somehow it feels like home.

Felix, confident with the fact there was no trouble the night before, and not one to miss out on a bit of revenue says we can stay there again, just one or two nights to start with but we can see how it goes.

The cafe sits on a Hill, or a big mound between the car park and the beach. Access to the cafe is made either via a driveway route up from the car park at the back, or up one of two steep wooden staircases one at either end leading up from the beach.

The cafe itself is built into a large open sided lorry trailer painted blue. At the front, facing the sea is the terrace. Two rows of wooden trestle benches and tables in various random colours. An arched metal frame holds up a ceiling of rolled out split bamboo for shade. It's generally not too busy, but there are times when it's absolutely rammed.

France, it seems, is quite a regimented country when it comes to food and drink and there are certain times when they must all do the same thing at the same time. I have not yet tuned into this. In fact, whenever in a large crowd I always seem to be walking in exactly the opposite direction to everybody else.

Where are they going? Why? Why now? Just a bit later I'll be walking along the same road and will be facing the crowds head on again. They move in waves. Although not too many French people in the mass of holidaymakers their psyche is preserved.

All I need to know is… 'When are the English on the beach?'

To the back of the cafe facing the car park a doorway has been cut. The door is always open to allow a through breeze. Felix's wife, whose name I know to be Annette, although I have never called her by it, always Madame, keeps a watchful eye on us from up there.

The old drum potato peeler rumbles away outback providing for an endless stream of frittes and there's a small cafe table with two slightly broken chairs and a Kroonenberg parasol that has seen better days. This is where we now do our nightly add-ups, known as 'le count'.

Our first day's work isn't encouraging. It's already hot as we gather under the trees with our co-workers. There are twelve of us, already too many for a van. There's us six, four very friendly and upbeat Algerians, and a German couple looking extremely nervous at the prospect of the drive.

We are all relieved when we see two vans pull in together, but this is short lived as when the back doors open we see there are already people in there, those who had camped on the farm and a few new faces. There are also stacks of polystyrene cool boxes and plastic bakers' trays filled with doughnuts. What the hell?

We all clamber in as best we can. The Germans think better of it and walk away quietly. Most of me wishing I had done the same thing.

The van isn't a sealed box, you can see the heads of the driver and two passengers in the front and if standing can see through the front windscreen. Both driver and passenger door windows are fully opened but it's hot in the back and getting hotter.

It's 20 minutes before the first drop off and we make the best of this time learning Algerian phrases and teaching English ones in return. It became apparent by their laughter that what they were teaching us wasn't what they were saying. After the first drop it's one every 5 or 10 minutes, the opening of the van doors giving no respite to the heat inside. Us newcomers it seems will be the last out.

Finally, it's my turn. I'm presented with a polystyrene ice box containing ice creams and canned drinks with a lump of dry ice to keep it cold, and a tray of doughnuts. There is a strap on either side to go behind my neck and hold the tray out flat in front of me. There's a small empty coffee cup with lid in the corner of the tray, this is to keep the money in, luckily for me I had some change in my pockets as a float.

The doors slam and the van tears away leaving

me standing there alone without a clue what I was doing. Where the hell is the beach? I take a few steps down a sandy track between two holiday homes.

No. Really? Stretching endlessly in either direction a virtually empty beach backed by holiday homes. Mostly stony with occasional patches of greyish sand. Perhaps a couple or a small family group every 100 yards or more. I compare it in my mind to the bustling beach I've just come from and despair.

I choose a direction and zig zag my way up the beach walking to each couple or group in turn and offering my wares, repeating the word Ben-yay as I had heard the day before.

I had Ben-yay nature, and ben-yay pomme In my tray, plain and apple doughnuts. You could call them doughnuts; they're made of the same stuff but they're not like any doughnut I've seen. Not round and perfect, but misshapen and long with slightly pointed ends, half of them filled with an apple compote.

I'm hungry and I try one even though I know it will cost me. I have to know what I'm selling. It's okay … I suppose. It's edible, not delicious though, a bit doughy and chewy, perhaps slightly undercooked or maybe this is just how they are. I was almost embarrassed by the last sale of the day, she clearly changed her mind when she saw it, but having called me over such a long way to the back of the beach felt obligated to buy it. For my part I just really needed the sale.

That day I spend five hours on the beach, my doughnuts open to the glaring sun getting less good with every passing hour. My total profit for the day 26 francs, roughly £2.60 and was surprised to get that, given an almost total lack of customers.

Here's how it works. Your employer will give you free of charge for example 20 Doughnuts 10 canned drinks and 10 ice creams. You sell whatever you can, and with your employer at the end of day count how many of each of these you have left. Deduct this from your mornings full quota and you have your day's sales.

You get to keep a percentage of each sale. You calculate what this is and give the rest of the cash, most of it, to your employer. Hopefully the sums will add up. Sometimes they don't. If you were to drop a doughnut in the sand, you'd have to pick it up, wrap it up and save it to prove you didn't sell it. There it is, Le count.

I sit and wait under a tree in the arranged spot.

Another beach seller emerges from the sandy path. He must have come from the opposite direction. I'm thinking that was lucky. He slumps down under the next tree about 30 feet away and we acknowledge each other.

Eventually a white van pulls up and we both stand, but this one has 'Richard' on the side, another company. He gets in, I sit back down. The driver gives me the eye as he pulls off, as if to say, 'you are not welcome on this beach'.

When my Gerard van pulls in its truly uninviting, but by this stage I just want to get back to camp and don't care.

My employer counts my remaining Doughnuts, drinks and ice creams and notes it down in his pad. He does a quick calculation, and I pay him what he asks from the pot, leaving me with my precious 26 francs plus float I started with. One by one as we pick up, we compare stories and takings.

It comes as no surprise that Jerry has taken more than me, but a bit of a surprise just how much more. To my 26 francs he has taken 38. The Canterbury 4 have taken between 8 francs, ouch, and 16 francs.

This pattern continues to this day, although the numbers are much bigger. Jerry's natural selling abilities give him a huge advantage and my desire to match puts me right up there. I absolutely know that this daily competition is what has driven me and made us both amongst a handful of the highest earners on the beach. Kings of the beach.

How far away this feels, like a different world. During that first day, in my mind I was already looking for an exit plan, after all I was in the South of France and making the break was the big thing, and I've done that. I absolutely know there are nicer looking places than this on the Mediterranean in either direction, down towards Spain or North and West the other way beyond Marseilles to the Cote D'Azur, but my wallet was low and unless I could earn money it was finite.

So, with the intention of building a reserve I stuck it out and glad I did. To be sat here now, calm, quiet and alone with the spectacle of the sand sea the sky, would be worth it on its own.

I can hear shouting and screams of laughter 100 yards or so down the beach. There is a large family group heading to the shoreline from what looks like the Italian campsite, the nearest campsite to us. They are carrying a young woman kicking and struggling. I'm pretty sure they aim to throw her in the sea. Yep, in she goes. Screams of laughter and lots of chasing going on. The sea is so calm that the ripples from the disturbance drift right down to me and right out to sea.

I take a slug from my beer, and the air is so still my

lighter doesn't even flicker as I re light my rollup I'd left to go out. I take a few steps to where the sea meets the beach. Even though the waves are barely an inch high they are enough to disturb a luminescent alga I have only seen once before.

Looking either way along the line of the waves there is an eerie bluey green glow like a faint luminous watch face. I wade in to my knees and the water glows around me. I disturb the water with my fingertips, and it glows around my fingers continuing to glow slightly on my hand after I've removed it from the water. It's an amazing sight. Otherworldly.

I think of going to tell the others but think better of it for the moment. This is nice, a perfect moment, I'm relaxed and feeling good, in fact in my life I can hardly remember feeling this good. Instead, I decide to take a dip.

Wow, the water is even warmer than the air and lighting up around me, some places brighter than others, some patches so bright that my hands and arms remain fully lit up out of water. Like a mutant superhero.

I swim for a bit, being careful to remain within my depth. It might look and even feel calm, but the currents here can be deceptive. You can go for a 10-minute swim and come out only to find your towel and stuff 100 yards up the beach, and it hasn't felt like you've moved anywhere.

Sometimes on a busy beach when the currents are strong people come out and think their stuff has been stolen as it's nowhere to be seen. The result being that as evening comes and everyone leaves, their lost possessions are just left sitting there on the beach.

Standing on tip toes, my head just above water I turn to face the land. In the sky there are the last remnants of a deep orange sunset, behind me is completely dark.

In one direction, south out of town towards Agde, it's dark for a good mile before you get to any civilisation. The beach is here backed by sand dunes, stretching inland, a nature reserve desperately clinging on as development encroaches from all directions. I can see a couple of beach campfires in the distance.

The other direction heading North towards town is just campsite on campsite lit up now as far as the eye can see.

The campsites by now have all started there round of nightly entertainment. For some this is just a small bar with perhaps a couple of musicians or generic euro pop playing through the small bar speakers, others provide a full-on nightlife with multiple night clubs and bars. Especially in the English section. I sometimes pop into these, not really my thing but can be fun. It is a good opportunity to catch up with your customers from the beach that day and perhaps make some new ones for the following.

From out here, in the water just beyond the beach I can see the distant white streetlights of the town of Sete twinkling in the warm night air. It might be just down the road but could be 1000 miles away. I've never been there, not even through it since those first couple of days in the van. Back then the beaches we were dropped at were well beyond. Places like Palavas and Valaras, just names now as I have no intention of returning.

I remember waking on that second day with a certain amount of trepidation. My back was still hurting from the weight of the tray the day before, and my neck sore from the strap, and for the £2.60 I'd made I didn't much fancy doing it again, But as we clambered out of the van the driver mentioned trying us on another beach tomorrow which he assured us would be an improvement, so with this in mind I decided to give it another shot. This was the general feeling; we'd give it another try.

It wasn't what we'd expected, but it was what it was, and it was what we'd come for.

After a quick swim, and a coffee and a sandwich for breakfast in the cafe that cost me almost half my previous day's takings I was ready for the off. Our driver was true to his word about changing beaches, this time we headed South. My drop off, although undoubtedly a more beautiful spot than the day before was equally deserted. To this day I don't know where that was, I was in the back both there and back so never saw the sign.

There were three sides of an old Spanish style town square with the fourth opening onto the beach and the sea beyond. In the square, shade was provided by rows of lowcut trimmed trees their branches knitted and twisted and growing together to form one continuous canopy.

Apart from a couple of cafes and the ubiquitous beach shop with buckets spades and inflated rubber dinghy's the place had hardly seemed to be hit by the tourist wave. This can't last long. I'm sure if I come back here in a few years' time it will have all changed. For now though, it's nice. If I didn't have the urgent need to make money this might be more the kind of place I'd head for.

It started much the same as the previous day, zigzagging from person to person, from group to group, then my first jackpot. Large French family group, perhaps two or three families together. They hail me over from the shoreline. By some great coincidence I just happened to be there at the exact moment when all French people eat. Doughnut time. Which is why there are doughnut sellers here in the first place.

Lesson learned, always try and catch this moment on a French beach. Time it right and you can empty your basket without an English person in sight. The downside being that the French beach sellers can time this moment perfectly, it's in their blood, and they hover around like sharks every few metres trying to do their entire business for the day in this moment.

The English, on the other hand buy steadily throughout the day whenever they get bored or hungry. Eating Doughnuts on a beach is a novelty and we play on that.

It's like fishing, they are not really interested in buying doughnuts, why would they be?, but we have to try and make them bite. First you get a nibble, some eye contact or a response to a call, then you have to reel them in. All too easy to let them off the hook, this is where the experience really lies.

On this occasion I sold no less than 10 Doughnuts 8 cans of drink and six ice creams. Bingo. Just in this moment I was beginning to see the appeal. Not only did it feel good, but it considerably lightened my load and gave me a fresh confidence for the day. Maybe, just maybe I might beat Jerry. After quickly picking up a few more sales in quick succession, my confidence boosted, I start to find my voice.

By now I'd come across a few other sellers and the standard call seemed to be 'der-mon-day' 'der-mon-day' 'ben-yay-o-pomme' ''ben-yay-nature 'der-mon-day'. Which basically translates as 'ask doughnuts' 'ask apple doughnuts'. Not very imaginative. I started calling B B B Beeeenyay. Like the woody woodpecker call. And 'Mmmm cest bon les ben-yay and 'probablement les meilleur ben-yay sur la plage' like the Heineken adverts. My terrible translations aimed at getting people smiling.

Like hitchhiking, I learned, you are more likely to get a lift if you smile, of course there is that 'what's he smiling at?' line not to cross.

I'd over stretched my distance so really had to get a pace on to get back to my pickup point, the van pulling up just moments after I arrived. I get encouraging sounds from my employer as he counts my returns. After settling up, my share remaining in the pot comes to a grand 42 francs. Less than I had calculated but still a good improvement on the day before. Next pick up Jerry. 58 francs. Doh, how did he do that?

The Canterbury four, had only fared marginally better than the previous day and were not quite so upbeat. There is no doubt about it, it's tough work. It's hot, and the sand is hot and burns at your ankles as you wade through it. The drinks in the cool box are heavy and the tray seems to weigh nothing when you put it on but pulls harder and harder on your shoulders as the day goes on even if it is getting lighter.

Back at camp Felix is watching down on us as we flop out around our tents. I see him gesturing me to join him in the cafe. I was just ready for a swim, but there's something about Felix, you just do what he says. In a good way, not that any harm would come to you If you didn't, you just want to make him happy, he's an important man and should be respected as such. What Felix says, goes.

Over time we would come to understand Just how important and respected he was, especially within the gypsy community, which is prominent in the area once you start to notice it and appreciate it.

Jerry and I join him at his table. This is where he is invariably to be found. In the shade with a large plastic bottle of ice-cold water. He gets it frozen from the freezer in the morning and drinks it as it slowly melts throughout the day. He's letting the next generation take the strain. Alain his son with his wife and toddler son mostly live on site in a small caravan at the end of the cafe wrapped in bamboo rolls to keep a low profile.

Probably none of us are supposed to be out here overnight, but they have stock and property to guard, and we are just chancing it by the day and lucky to be here.

Alain's cousin Bernat, and his wife Sylvie also work here. They have four children who are everywhere at all times throughout the day. They are charming and well behaved, just very active. It's always somewhat of a relief, and a calm descends when they head off home in the evening.

So, Felix asks, what is it you lot do? Are you working? We Tell him the whole Story, the party in Canterbury and now we've come here to sell doughnuts on the beach. He pauses for thought, even stops me from talking with the slightest raise of a finger. He's an imposing character, dark weathered skin with thick combed back grey hair and bushy grey walrus moustache.

He plays with his moustache as he ponders then leans forward both hands flat out on the table and says, with his strong Catalan accent what I understand to be 'Now you work for me. Right here on this beach'. I go into translation mode for Jerry who gets some of it, but the accent takes some getting used to.

His offer was to provide us, just as now with doughnuts and ice creams and drinks to sell on the beach. It was a very tempting offer indeed, although it was less of an offer than a statement. It was a no brainer. No morning travel, and a beach we knew to be busy and seemed to get consistently busier as it went. The offer was for all six of us and the icing on the cake was free camping as long as we were working. What's to lose we thought, and shake on it, feeling sure the others would be good with this. He explains it'll take him a few days to prepare properly and arrange a reliable supply of doughnuts.

The only slightly concerning thing was that as we were leaving, he added, 'Of course, if anyone were to ask you who you work for...' and tapped his nose. Basically, it meant this probably wasn't strictly speaking licensed and legal, and that if we got caught, we'd be on our own.

The following day, three of the Canterbury 4 decide to take some time out and wait for their new job to start, leaving Jerry me and Bill to head off to the van partly with the feeling of loyalty not wanting to let them down. When we got to the van, ready to make up a story and apologise for the others not being there it turned out they weren't even slightly bothered, and no explanation necessary.

They work on such a high turnover of disillusioned adventurers that they would hardly notice especially given their low sales record. This made me feel better about letting them down tomorrow as this was almost certainly my last day of this too.

I get the same beach as the day before and quite a few fortunate early sales, then what at first seems to be disaster. The post secure, kind of lifeguard meets beach police, have spotted me possibly on a beach I shouldn't have been on, how would I know? and have reported me to the actual police now parked at the top of the beach and beckoning me towards them. They demand my name, and who it is I work for. Now I start to understand Felix's comment.

I tell him my name and that I worked for Gerard. They are not happy about this. They take my tray of doughnuts and shake the contents into a large flip top bin, then empty the contents of my cool box into a plastic bag and put it into the boot of their car. Leaving me with just my block of dry ice.

I speak a bit of French, but in this case pretend not to. However, as they scribble out the ticket to prove to my boss this has happened, I understand well that they never want to see me here again. Don't worry I'm thinking, you won't.

What happens now? Only one hour out of five and nothing to sell, all gone in an instant.

Cool, day off. I stash my empty tray and cool box under some decking on the beach and takings in hand head off to one of the terrace cafes in the square. I'd sold about 8 doughnuts, a couple of cans and three ice creams, so I had quite a bit of cash.

While sipping on an ice-cold beer from a stemmed glass pondered 'what if I'd only sold two? How would they know? I scrutinised the ticket the police had given me it had scrawled my name their name the offence and the time it happened, it turns out only 40 mins into my shift, and that goods had been seized, but no mention of what goods or quantity of goods.

I was pretty damn sure Gerard wasn't going to go to the local police station and insist on counting the cans they'd seized. And the doughnuts were just in a stinking bin along with everything else... uncountable.

There was my plan, I didn't feel great about it and was a bit nervous about pulling it off but on the other hand I could justify it by the fact I was almost and could have been arrested and they must have known I wasn't even supposed to be there.

After a nice day on the beach with a swim, lunch and a few beers, when the van finally arrived, I just told them I'd sold the two doughnuts and one drink, making sure the money in the cup tallied with that settled up with the rest tucked away in my pocket. I saw it as my golden handshake for my many hours of low paid loyal service.

Jerry had done ok again, and Bill had stepped up a bit, but we all agreed while being bounced about in the back of an airless hot van that this was a mugs game. I leave it until just before the van pulls off before I call out 'sorry, we won't be here tomorrow'. OK he says. Like 'am I bothered?'. Funny enough, with skulduggery, this has been the only day I have topped Jerry's beach earnings.

What seems so everyday now was so alien back then, it still makes me smile that I did that, so unlike me, the me that was. It wasn't so long ago, it can be counted in weeks, but each day so full the experience seems more like months, years even. I'm swimming in the same spot but am in a very different place.

I swim into the shore and sit in the shadows, lapping waves at my feet still glowing in the water. The water is warm, but the air now feels slightly warmer. Sitting here alone like this is just heaven.

I'm about 100 yards down the beach from the cafe just down in the darkness. Looking back, I can see the string light bulbs are still on and there were some people eating or drinking on the terrace. I'm aware of them in the light, but I'm far enough down that they are not aware of me.

I usually walk this far down to be not immediately in their view. To disappear into the numbers during the day or the darkness in the evening and at night.

The Sky is now fully dark and full of stars. A deep red moon Is rising from the sea, its reflection comes toward me on the glassy now black sea and stops right at my feet, still glowing green. Wow, this is amazing, like being on another planet.

I feel I should go and get the others to share these natural wonders and to this avail I wonder back up to my tattered beach mat and clothes but end up sitting down and turning back towards the moon. This moment, it seems is for me.

I pull my shirt over my shoulders. The night is just now starting to feel a bit fresher, the first real relief from the heat of the day, and you can visually see the occasional very light breeze as it disturbs the otherwise glassy sea.

The moon is taking on an orange tint as it rises before my eyes, sitting balanced on the horizon like a yellow snooker ball, and the column, still pointing directly at me is getting brighter and shimmering in the breezes, some of which are out to sea and come nowhere near the land.

It's a spectacle, and I would waste it by running down the beach to tell the others. I'll just sit here and enjoy it. Beer is still freezing although the lump of beer ice has now gone and time for that other rollup. Luckily, I remembered to drop it in my hat before heading into the sea.

Having those few days off between jobs was a god send. A few days to chill, and for those that didn't, to get to know each other. It was a chance to discover our environment and where we had landed and to recce the beach we would be working on.

We also had a chance to set our camp up properly, to move the tents and camper around with a low profile in mind. It was only a car park, so not much to look at, but it was empty at night and the location was just perfect, sleeping at night to the sound of Mediterranean lapping waves.

We move our camp in closer to the one storey house to make the most of its concrete patio. It's good to get off the sand. We spend a day clearing it of old boxes and trolleys and various other items of scrap metal which we tidy into a pile behind the house and cover with an old green tarpaulin weighted down with stones.

After sweeping off the mounds of accumulated sand we finally hose it down and it's ready to use. All under the watchful eye of the Gypsies on the hill. Well, they haven't stopped us, so they must be okay with it.

There are still junk remnants of the old campsite lying about in corners and we manage to construct a nice table out of two broken ones and gather some almost usable chairs. These all get a good hose down, in this place fine sand dust covers everything.

Jerry draws his camper along the end of our new patio and hangs the speakers on the doors. We've arrived.

We can't use the house itself, but this is surely the next best thing. As for the house, it's one window, and single door firmly shut and locked, with sand accumulation making it appear they haven't been opened this year.

Next morning, after a leisurely breakfast 'a table', Jerry and I are keen to check out the beach, and tired of waiting for the others who are clearly going to be sometime say we'll meet them later and head on out. This is a pattern that is also repeated. Always Jerry first, then me, I can never beat him, and then the others sometime later. I've never known when they hit the beach, I'm not there.

You soon learn, if you are walking distances on beaches that the easiest place to walk is where the waves lapped the sand, 'the hard shoulder' as we call it. It's cooler and firmer under foot and you can get a good pace on, only leaving it to make a sale. Until the English beach that is.

It's about 10am and the beach is steadily filling, compared to the beaches we've been working on it's already busy. It's hot and getting hotter. The Gypsies have told us that even by local standards these last few days, since we have been here have been exceptional. Too hot, I've heard said several times. But not for me, at least not yet.

As we walk, we can work out where one campsite ends and another begins, with the occasional punctuation of a beach cafe usually placed at the end of the main walking routes from town. We can't see into the campsites as there is a tall bank of sand at the back of the beach with well-trod sandy paths leading down from them.

But we can see flags, and for the first time get the sense that these campsites are catering for individual nationalities. First Italian, then German for a good long stretch, at least two campsites, French for another good stretch, Dutch, German again, then a few hundred yards of mixed before… ta da, English.

It took a good few weeks to work this out properly and it's backed up by the different languages you hear on the beach along the way. Jerry and I go on to fully maximise this knowledge learning to call our wares in every language.

After walking for a good 25 minutes we still haven't reached, and have as yet no knowledge of the English beach. We decide to wade up the beach through the hot sand to a small cafe with the few parasoled tables on decking at the top of the beach. It's a busy spot, a main on-foot beach route from town.

We order a couple of cokes, nicely served with ice and lemon in a glass, and sit at a table to watch the scene. This has become one of my favourite spots. A nice midway stop off whichever way you are headed.

There is a steady flow from town as the beach continues to fill, amongst them come four doughnut sellers in a group that split off like the Red Arrows when they hit the beach. Already they are not looking happy, a bit scruffy and unshaven like they've been sleeping rough.

Each of them has the same cry, the familiar dermondy dermondy ben yay boison fresh. It's like they've been told to say that, and nobody wants to stray from the script. They have the same trays and boxes we had had, so we surmise they work for Gerard, and we have seen other sellers on the beach with basket trays that we believe to be Richard.

Gerard and Richard certainly seem to be the biggest competition on the beach, and we don't think they're going to take well to another six independent sellers, although that's not our problem. Drinks finished we head back to the hard shoulder and continue our quest. We are wondering, with all these nationalities if there will be an English beach? It would certainly make life easier not to have to translate, and for a bit of banter.

After another 10 minutes, approximately half an hour from our base, we start to see, can it be? Yes, in the distance a row of Union Jack flags hanging in the hot still air.

Normally if I were to see these on holiday, I would run a mile, but this time they drew us in like magnets. It was a different mindset. We weren't holiday makers; we were here to stay, to survive and maybe even prosper, and yet it has always seemed like a holiday. Enough of our time is spent on swimming eating drinking and having fun to keep it that way.

We finally reach it and decide to explore off the beach. We've been walking along wading through the shallow water, I have my sandals in hand and for the first time make the big mistake of walking across the now burning hot sand barefoot. Ow ow ow, a quick hop and jump back to the water to cool them off and sandals on. Even with sandals it can get uncomfortable especially towards the end of a long day when it whips up and stings your heels as you walk.

We look back down the beach to see how far down we have walked. The café is in view, in that it's a straight beach, but too far to recognise or pick out any detail. This distance... from there, to here, will be our daily commute, working as we go through all nations and trying to catch the French doughnut moment.

Looking up that way now it's easy to see how far it is. There's a big searchlight shining from a nightclub which combes the air as if looking for aeroplanes. The nightclub, I can hear even from here, is in an enclosed open-air courtyard space. It goes on until about midnight then a couple of smaller indoor clubs takeover to the early hours.

It can be fun, but there are better nights to be had, and there are often small breakouts of trouble. Mostly posturing, but the occasional full-on fight which is never nice to be around. It's a different world down there.

The breezes are picking up, becoming cooler and more frequent. I notice that as they disturb the surface of the water they cause the luminescence to glow in patches. The moon, now fully above the horizon is now much brighter, almost white, and yet looks somehow smaller. The column of reflection still pointing directly towards me, but the whole sea now has a silvery surface.

Arriving here now seems so long ago, but the day Felix presented us with our doughnuts feels like yesterday. Wow. Really? These were in a different league to the doughnuts the others were selling. Straight out of a patisserie window. Felix has done a deal with a local gypsy baker in Agde who has agreed to provide us with as many as we need.

He puts the tray on our table, there are about twenty in there, apple and custard, and gestures us try them. I go for custard. Oh my god… that is amazing. Definitely and by far the best doughnut I've ever tasted.

Evenly golden and light, about 5 or 6 inches long sliced down the middle with a generous piping of custard or apple compote. The custard is delicious, the doughnut amazing. I still eat one every morning before work. Here we have a big advantage on the other sellers. This was really high-quality food against their misshapen blobs of either burnt or undercooked dough.

Until this trip I'd never really met any Gypsies, certainly not to talk to. My experience here has been a real eye-opener. Our family have proved to be close loving and caring. They care for each other, and they care for others. Annette has been looking after us since we arrived.

They never encroach on our space, rarely do they come down to our camp and never complain when we push it a bit on the party front. We may get a disapproving glance in the morning but generally it's live and let live. They do well from us, and we do well by them.

Part of my job for Felix is to find new workers for the beach. About a month ago a drifter wandered into the car park. He was filthy and looked a bit drunk. To me he looked beyond the pale, his glasses were so greasy I could hardly see his eyes, but he actually asked me if I knew of any work, so I had to mention him to Felix a bit embarrassed to do so.

When Annette saw him she insisted on feeding him. A big hearty meal of her home-made lamb stew which is normally reserved for the family and not on the menu, with frittes on the side.

Later that day they took him back to their home and gave him a chance to wash and wash his clothes and get himself together. A few days later they brought him back a different person. Still a bit vague and distant, but clean and with shiny glasses and the beginnings of an emergent smile.

He is still here; he collects glasses and generally

helps out around the café. He is English but speaks fluent French and is a bit chattier now. Although we still know virtually nothing about him, we're starting to see the man he used to be. The gypsies saw this immediately. He was in need of help, and they helped him. Felix wants to start him on the beach soon but he's clearly happy where he is.

Our place can become a magnet for lost souls. We are right at the end of town, the very last thing, so it's just where they end up. Valérie was one of these. She wandered in early evening a couple of weeks back looking somewhat bewildered. She had no bags or belongings of any kind. She was clearly at a loss, so I invited her to join us at out table. Over some food her tale of the day's events unfolded.

She had been hitching not far from Marseille and had picked up a great lift that brought here almost to here. The driver was a really nice guy, and they chatted and got on well the whole journey. To her it had seemed like the beginning of something.

It had been the hottest of days and he suggested they stop for a swim. He pulled into a carpark about half a mile short of town and they went down to the water. He made an excuse of going back to the car to grab his towel and never came back. He just drove off with all her belongings leaving her with nothing.

Traumatised and still utterly disbelieving she just started walking until ending up here. The women leant her some clothes and I gave her my tent I was no longer using, and she stayed. She's working on the beach and doing ok. Her smile is back now. Every day is her last but she's still here. There is something about this place.

She has a striking appearance, and it turns out she is a model. Her biggest loss in the theft, the irreplaceable one, was her models folio that had cost her thousands to put together. She had been on her way to an interview in Spain with it, but of course never made it.

I can see a figure along the beach in the half light from the campsites. He seems to be zigzagging from shoreline to the back of the beach. It must be Willie on his nightly rounds. Willie is a nice guy, he's in his 30s, a total old school hippy. He now lives in the area year-round in Marseillan Ville.

He has a really nice old house with a courtyard just on the edge of town. We went there for the night recently but before going inside he confessed he has a cockroach infestation. He says he's waiting for the council to come round but in the meantime good practise is to turn the lights on and burst into the room stamping on as many as possible before they disappear into the darker corners. The more the merrier. This we do, expecting to see them everywhere but there are only two or three and these are quickly dispatched. Crunch, crunch, crunch.

As the Storey goes, Willie used to be a beach seller way back in the day, when there were only two or three on the beach. From the days when Marsellian Plage was literally a quaint seaside spot, before the development set in. In those days, he tells us, the campsites were all small family affairs, just like the gypsy's campsite. One by one they have become the overblown hotel sites they are today.

One Day while sitting on the beach by total chance he uncovered a small puddle of money. Nothing valuable, just change but it made him think if this one is here, they must be everywhere. You Have your holiday shorts on, with change in your pocket and as you sit down it slips out onto the sand and, as everything does, immediately disappears below the surface. It's right there next to you but you don't know it's gone. Hence the phenomenon of money puddles.

A change of career was in hand. He put down his doughnut tray and purchased a metal detector. He's been doing that ever since. Maybe 10 years or more. He's not rich, but it provides him with enough to sustain him and he's happy. Occasionally he'll find a ring, or a gold necklace that swings the balance in his favour. I always like to chat with him, but it doesn't look like he's coming this far down. In fact, looking again he's probably gone up to our place.

'Our place'… that is so cool. Our own place in the South of France right on the beach. It's really starting to come together now. A good few weeks ago I built up the courage to ask Felix 'What's in the house? '. Living outside it was great but I was dying to know what was inside. And in my wildest dreams get my hands on a key.

Sat at his table, Felix knows exactly why I'm asking as obviously it would be a step up from a tent. I used the pretext 'If we had the key, it would be handy for locking stuff away, like cash'. And could be somewhere to store our trays and cool boxes that we were presently hiding away each night in case of a visit from the authorities.

To my astonishment he stands, which is quite rare in itself, and walks to the cafe to pick a bunch of keys off the hook board. I follow him down the back drive, the others see us coming and quickly tidy up. After fumbling through a few keys finally one fits and as he turns it twice in the lock I'm thinking yes! It's all going to change now.

The door creaks open and needs a bit of a shove. There is no power, says Felix, so we peer into the darkness. It's full, full of stuff, cafe stuff, pots and pans piles of old plates, and campsite stuff, old signage and piles of boxes. We pick our way through.

Felix opens the side window and struggles to unlock and open the rusted metal shutters. As they swing open light floods in. It's like a building that was never really finished, before being hijacked as a storage space. perhaps they had a plan to use it in the glory days of the campsite.

It's essentially one big room with a dividing wall down the middle and a doorway connecting the two halves. The room we are in has the front door and a side window. The other room I'm picking my way towards through the clutter has one window that leads onto our patio. I poke my head through the door into the darkness and I'm thinking '*my room*'.

After a few crashes and bangs in the dark I manage to open the front window. As I unfold the complaining shutters there is my new view. Patio tents and camper in the foreground, cafe on the hill just to my right, and directly in front an expanse of deep blue Mediterranean Sea. If only I can persuade Felix.

My offer to Felix, to completely clean it out inside and out in exchange for being able to use it on occasion. To the back of the building is a breeze block tin roofed extension. Apart from the chest freezer it's more or less empty.

I make the quick calculation everything I see in these rooms could be neatly stacked away in there. A good deal of it would go straight under the junk tarpaulin which was growing daily as we gradually cleared the car park and its perimeters. Until one day last week that is when we got back from the beach to find it was gone. They had finally cleared it.

I offer Felix a drink, we have some small water bottles cooling in the chest freezer. He accepts and joins us for the first time at our table. He's smiling. I think he's getting a picture of how it used to be in the days of the campsite and is genuinely pleased for us to be there. It's a bit of a moment.

Okay he says looking me in the eye, something along the lines of don't 'touché Mon bit' which I took to translate as 'don't pull my plonker, or 'take the mickey'. He was Reminding me that he was the boss around here and that if he were to give us this inch, we shouldn't take the mile. I had at least half a mile in mind and of course he knew this.

So there it was. The house, in the South of France. Quite an achievement. But at that moment it was a daunting task. Felix removes that key from the ring and presses it into my palm with his thumb. Without words is saying I'm trusting you with this and the responsibility is all yours. Don't let me down. I didn't plan to. I would make him proud.

As Felix heads on back up the slope, with a shiver of excitement key still firmly in hand I take another step across the threshold. Oh my God, I was shaking. I never thought this would happen. So cool. Looking around me... boxes, I was going to need boxes and lots of them... and help, it would take forever doing this on my own.

All I'm really after is the bedroom, that's the bit I've got my eye on. The other room with the door I was happy for everyone to use as a communal space. We'd probably have a table and a bit of a kitchen in there. With no power it will always be candle and lamp lit... then it strikes me. Extension lead from the lean-to. The freezer must be running on something. I keep this idea to myself for a bit, I don't want to jump in too quick and upset Felix by lighting it up like a Christmas tree.

It turns out boxes in this town are easy to find. The place runs on them. Endless deliveries of tourist consumables. Behind every store or cafe front there is a mountain of them, and the owners are only too pleased for you to take them away. Me Jerry and Bill collect a few camper vans full from just down the lane and start the long process of packing and labelling.

Pots and pans, and in a separate box, lids, as none of them seem to fit the pots. Plates, cups, cutlery, kitchen utensils, some of this would be useful to us too. Gradually, bit by bit, box by box, all watched over from the hill, the house empties and the storeroom fills.

Some of this stuff we're moving I would really like to buy off them and take back to London although have no way of doing this. Some of the old signs are stylish. There is one in particular, a box light, the word Bienvenue in red italic letters on a golden yellow background.

It would have originally lived on a pole by the entrance. Not quite rectangle, stretched upwards and outwards at the top, 60s style. It's back now missing it has two light fittings inside with no bulbs. I decided to keep this one aside to clean and use, maybe put a battery lamp in.

I can hear music coming from our place now. I know it's from there because it's Jerry playing 'Space Cowboy', the extended disco mix, he'll be dancing around by the speakers.

Jerry can be infuriating at times, and can absolutely drive me crazy beating me to the beach, but he's also a great guy, a good friend and fun to be around. Things happen because of him, like this. I wouldn't be here without him, and I will always be grateful, and although at work we can be the fiercest of rivals we have each others back.

I think of heading back but instead decide to take a walk along the beach down into the darkness following the shoreline.

Some of the luminescence has gone now, but it's still bright in places like a dotted 'cut here' line. Barefoot I disturb the water in these places causing green pools to appear as I look back some of them are still glowing.

It's not cold, but it's not warm either. Way down the beach I can see a glimmer of a campfire and I decide to make that my destination. I'll chance it and see who's by it. I might be welcome, I might not. The people down this way out of town are generally chilled.

When you are living just yards from the Mediterranean you get a sense of its moods. It's so rarely this calm. It has virtually no tide, apart from on a full moon when incredibly the sea can reach the top of the beach. It's generally not that rough, although can have its moments and, although mostly blue has endless variations of hue from a brilliant bright turquoise to a jet-black rumbling monster with white crests and crashing waves that can sweep you off your feet. Although it's mood is mostly linked to the weather it can throw up surprises of its own, like tonight's spectacular light show.

I only know a couple of people down this way. There is a campsite way down and I know the security guards. They sometimes park in the carpark and have breakfast at the cafe before walking down the beach to work. They became quite good friends and used to stop by after work at the end of their shifts. I keep them at arm's length now after a recent experience I won't forget in a hurry.

I had been heading down when I saw them talking to another couple of guys at the top of the beach where the campsite meets the beach. They look like they were having a good chat and from a distance it looks light-hearted. I wander up to say hi and just as I get there it turns ugly.

It turns out my friends were trying to eject them from the campsite, and they didn't want to leave.

After a few quick movements, not even a scuffle, out of nowhere my friend produces an aerosol of CS gas, teargas. Points it and lets it off right in their faces and they drop... but there was a strong wind from behind and it catches me too, full on in the face.

Man that stuff hurts. It took me a few minutes before I could properly see again and my nose and throat, eyes and ears we're burning. The blowback also caught both of my friends, but to a lesser degree.

Their big lesson learned, if you intend to use teargas, make sure you're pointing downwind. My lesson learnt, stay away from gits with tear gas! The guys it was aimed at took it full on, it must have been extreme. It's a vicious weapon to use and to my mind he used it way too lightly.

I had to take the next day off, my first since working for Felix, and It took me several days to fully shake the effects. I don't know...call me old fashioned.... but it is hard to be friends with someone who is tear gassed you. He's been really apologetic ever since, but hmmm. Naa.

I continue walking towards the fire, but it doesn't seem to be getting nearer. Eventually I'm close enough to see three people sitting around it. As I approach, they turn and welcome me. I was hoping for a chat with some chilled holiday makers, but that's not what I got.

The beach is like a magnet for the transient, people who spend the whole year moving around Europe looking for work, or a way to survive. Some, like us work hard, others have chosen an easier lifestyle of begging and others, stealing. Some are lost souls. They have had their confidence and dignity stripped from them by the sometimes-brutal lifestyle. They are survivors, just trying to get by.

I join them at their fire, trying to get the measure of them. They are clearly not anything to do with the campsite further down and have come this far into the darkness just to find a place to be, not disturbed by the authorities. Each has an old sleeping bag, and their plan seems to be to sleep here.

I'm cagy when they ask where I am staying, I just say "Oh, down that way". While we chat, a dog appears from over the dune leading to the campsite. It has a big slab of meat in its mouth and tail is wagging as he gorges on it, covered in sand as it is. 'Well done boy' one of them says, you've managed to find some food. 'Good boy, yes you are.'

I ask what they are up to.

"We beg", one of them exclaims proudly. I'm supposed to be impressed. I have nothing against beggars here, it's just a method of survival and often how people first put their feet down. It's not an identity, just something they've fallen into, it beats hunger. But there is something about this lot I'm not comfortable with, it's all a bit edgy.

"Cool", I say, but I'm looking for a way to make my exit.

"We share this little guy", referring to the dog. "You always get more if you have a dog with you" he continues, "So we share him."

I don't want to push it, but I'm intrigued how much they can make. I ask. It turns out they make up to fifty francs a day, a fiver between them, "And whatever we can nick."

"How so?" I ask. Seeming to have my confidence, one of them tells me, "Well, tents aren't exactly safes."

He adds, 'Holidaymakers are such mugs. They hide their money in their sleeping bags when they go to the beach thinking this will make it harder to find, but I have my secret weapon.' He unfolds a wooden-handled pen knife. 'All you have to do is slit the tent and bag from the end and hey presto.'

I'm thinking, rotten bastards I was right to be wary. There's another holiday ruined.' Time to leave.

"I don't suppose you have any spare cash?" one of them asks as I stand. He's smiling but still feels a bit threatening.

"Sorry mate, skint" is my best reply

It seems every seaside town like this one has its official workers, bar staff, waiters and waitresses, shopkeepers, DJs, deckchair renters and so on. But there is also us, a hidden community of 'unofficial' workers, without whom the system wouldn't work. We do all the other stuff.

Beach work, we have discovered is the best of all jobs, especially if you take it as seriously as we do, but people will do anything to survive and take on any job that comes along. Cheap and cash in hand. We have a mutual respect, or at very least a tolerance, but all agree we'd be better off without the thieves. They give us all a bad name.

We keep our distance, always letting others in our community know who they are when we come across them. Those who steal from shops and businesses are tolerated, hunger is hunger, it's just those who steal from individuals, tourists, that are universally looked down on by all, 'Bastards'.

We have a good friend 'Charlie', who does very well selling sandwiches on the beach these days but proudly tells of how he started by stealing ham and cheese from the supermarket by sticking them down in his pants, and just buying the cheaper element, bread, not so easy to conceal, then making them into sandwiches for sale on the beach. Little did his unsuspecting punters know.

He could have just made sandwiches to eat himself but didn't because A. it had been down his pants, and B. a sandwich can sell on the beach for up to eight franks, just selling a couple was enough to live on.

After a week or so, now with money in his pockets he was buying his ingredients as the risk grew with every day, and hey, he could afford it. He tells us two franks can be turned into eight just by making a sandwich and walking 100 yards with it.

Sometimes I'll swap a doughnut for one while out working. These days they are good, he makes a good sandwich, ham salad mayonnaise and cheese salad, both designed for the English market. You can't live on doughnuts alone, but can never totally be sure it hasn't seen his pants. It's an ongoing joke.

I start the long dark walk back along the beach towards the lights and our place. I check behind a couple of times to make sure I'm not being followed, I'm not. I had gone further than I had thought and so rather than struggling across soft sinking sand I head for the water's edge where the sand is firm and I can get a good pace on.

Eventually I'm close enough to see the Gypsies' café, the lights are still on which is unusual at this time in the evening and can hear 'Feeling Hot Hot Hot' the big hit from last year's Notting Hill Carnival, drifting towards me, so someone has put on one of my mix tapes, it's a good one, my best.

I was at carnival last year, and it was, as the song has it, Hot Hot Hot, it played everywhere, from steel bands to carnival floats it just really fitted the mood of the occasion. I remember that as being one if the best days ever.

It was my third carnival and there was an extra something about this one, the combination of glorious sunshine and that song, that truly lifted my spirits. With just so much noise, distraction, music and humanity, there is, nothing else like it and somehow in that environment I get to be me.

I had another taste for freedom, me-dom, back in June which is probably the real reason I'm here. A friend Steve and I took a random trip to Stonehenge Free Festival, my first festival. Three days were nowhere near enough, I wanted it to last forever. It was a glimpse into another alternative world, my world, which wasn't the world I was headed back to, so something was going to give, and it was this.

It's not even something others would notice, I've got friends and a good social life. I see live music most weeks and hope to become a musician, and I can keep down a job. It's more of a me thing, a disconnect, life just seems easier for other people. 'Alternative' surrounding just fit me better.

I don't walk straight up, instead I pass on the beach and look over to see who is there. I can make out about ten or fifteen people sitting around our long table. It looks nice but I'm not quite ready for it. I'm still enjoying a bit of time out.

I decide to take one last swim, it's still warm enough and the sea is calling me in. The temperature of the water again feeling warmer than the night air. I continue out until I'm on my toes, there being no waves, and with the salinity of the water I just enjoy floating and wading up to my neck with a feeling of weightlessness.

There is no feeling like it, all the time keeping half an eye on the dark blob that is my clothes and mat in the moonlight, making sure no one approaches them, especially with the knowledge there are thieves on the beach tonight.

A big group of people have just wandered onto the beach, I'm a way off but it looks like they are coming this way. I wade out and make my way up the beach towards the carpark, I'm glad I did. They are, it sounds like all men, maybe German?, about 15 of them, loud and staggering drunk, and hanging onto each other for support.

Slightly aggressively one of them shouts out to me. I wave, as if I've understood and keep walking, picking up my pace a bit. He shouts again, I smile and reply 'alright mate?' He gives up, god knows what he was trying to say. There's a bit of shouting, I hear the word 'English' so I guess it's aimed at me. Fortunately, they turn and head up beach, towards the campsites.

Looking towards our house I can see a figure walking towards the beach. Silhouetted by the lights behind I make out that is Cassie by the way her hair is piled up on her head. I call out 'hey Cass'. Her eyes not yet adjusted I can see she is looking for the source of my voice, I wave.

She works with us on the beach, coming as many do as a holiday maker then simply staying on after the two weeks is up. She came with her fiancé but didn't want it to end, he wasn't so adventurous and went home, and I got her a job with the Gypsies. She's started to do quite well. Being a bit on the quiet side she will never make as much and Jerry and me, but she gets by.

Cassie earns a bit of extra money claiming to have invented the bottle scam. Most of us already knew it but we let her take the credit. Bottles, it turns out are refundable for cash at the mini market tills. These lie diagonally to each other, and each has a crate for returned bottles. The scam, if you can get someone to distract the person on checkout you can simply pick up one of these full cases, lifting it from one checkout to the next and claim the money.

It could otherwise take a full hour or two to fill one legitimately, this way it's done in an instant 'earning' a cool five franks for the full case, then back round to the entrance to spend it in the shop. The perfect crime. One time, with a bunch of us, the same crate moved like this across all four checkouts earning us twenty franks to share.

Because we didn't actually leave the shop with anything, except the cash, it didn't really feel like stealing, I mean they give you the money, and the worst that could happen is you'd get spotted doing it, which on the one time this occurred just resulted in being thrown out of the shop. With a fast turnaround of cashiers, we were back at it within the week.

"Where have you been?" Cassie asks.

"Oh, just down the beach, chilling. The sea was glowing green earlier, did you see it?"

"No, you should have come and got me."

"Sorry, I got lost in the moment."

"I came looking," she says. "Sorry, I took a walk down the beach, bumped into some scallies at a fire. Bad-uns. Were you looking for a particular reason?"

"No, just fancied some time out, but I'm not mad about being on the beach on my own at night. Especially with scallies about."

"I just had a moment myself, did you hear that lot?" Looking down the beach, the Germans are a fair distance now. "I thought that was my lot for a moment. I was ready to outrun them."

We sit on the beach and look out to sea.

"Have you noticed," I say, "how the beach is always clean in the morning? All stripey, as if it's been raked."

"I know, it's weird. I've never seen anyone do it. If it's a machine, you'd think we would hear it, I mean we are just there."

"Last week we were at that table just there until after dawn. I had about three hours sleep before work. By the time I got up for a morning dip, it was all done, the whole beach. It's miles long, how the hell do they do that?"

"If we stood here long enough, I guess we'd find out."

"I quite like the mystery."

"How'd you do today?" Cassie asks.

"Not too bad, not great, it's just too hot for people to spend that long on the beach. You have to catch them quick. I took about a hundred and forty all told."

"You call that not bad? I took sixty. Nearly all in drinks. Who the hell would want a doughnut in that heat?"

"That's your job to convince them they do. Mad, isn't it? Of all things to sell, doughnuts, I mean what the hell? Whose idea was that?"

"Tradition."

"Not ours. We just tell them, this is what you eat here and they believe it."

"So you are happy? Glad you stayed?" I ask.

"Sure, so glad, I wouldn't miss this for the world. I mean, it's messed my life up completely. My fiancé has left me, accused me of having an affair... with you of all people."

"Thanks."

"Sorry," she laughs. "You know what I mean. "

I didn't, but hey, I smile.

"And to cap it all" she continues, "I phoned my job today and they have fired me."

"Oh, sorry to hear it."

"Not me, I hated it, I didn't even realize, I just went through the motions. Everyone told me it was so great, such a great opportunity, but it doesn't beat this."

"My work couldn't believe it either. I was a groundsman in a posh school. I could have spent today sitting on a tractor, going up and down, just so young toffs can play cricket. I can't stand cricket… or young toffs… or schools come to that."

I ask, "So what will you do when you get home?"

"Haven't thought about it much. Not sure I'll go home. If this has shown me anything, it's that life can hold surprises. I never in a million years thought I'd do this, until I met you."

"Hey, don't blame me, it was your choice, you came asking if I remember rightly."

"No, not blaming, thanking you I guess." She smiles "…probably, let's see how it turns out"

"How's your love life?" she asks, smiling, and carries on, "Didn't I hear something about you and Kylie from Milton Keynes?"

"She should be so lucky. Don't believe a word of it. That's what she went around telling everyone, she didn't think to ask me. Anyway, she has properly got the hump with me now."

"How so?"

"You didn't hear?"

"No, hear what? Spill all."

"Round at their camp in the woods the other night. There were a few of us sitting around the fire and she came and sat next to me. Out of politeness, just something to say, I asked, 'What are you up to later?' She came back with 'I'm sleeping with you,', and everyone is all ooooh. But I'm thinking, no you're bloody not."

"Is that why she's pissed off?"

"Not in itself, the problem was as I thought it, I said it out loud, and everyone thought it was hysterical. Everyone but Kylie, she stormed off."

"Ouch."

"Ouch nothing. If I had a car, she'd have slashed my tyres by now. "

Sharing my scrap of beach mat, heels in the sand, we stare out to sea to the familiar sound of soft lapping waves. From behind us 'Welcome to the House of Fun' drifts down from Jerry's speakers, it seems apt.

I notice the waves, only an inch or two tall, but

from none only a couple of hours ago. Maybe the sea telling me something.

At nighttime on the far horizon you can make out container and cruise ships heading I guess to and from Marseille. You can tell the cruise ships as they are lit up brightly. At first, they seem static, but if you look away for a bit, they move quite fast and in no time are gone from view.

The moon is now high and giving off plenty of light, no need for a torch, lucky as I haven't got one. Lights are still on up at the café, strange, and light the beach in front of them. Jerry's mix tape moves on to 'The Message' 'Don't push me cos I'm close to the edge…'. Here I couldn't be further from it.

This, being out here in the evening is still my favourite thing to do here. All the rest of it facilitates this. Life here is fun, more than fun, but it's busy, hectic, sometimes dangerous and often exhausting, and this? this is more or less perfect. I guess I need both, one compliments the other.

To think within 1 mile of here are literally thousands, tens of thousands of holiday makers, and yet we are the only ones appreciating this scene. They are missing the best bit.

"I'm getting thirsty now. C'mon, let's go and join

the others and grab a cold beer," I suggest. "I've got some stashed at the back of the freezer, should be just about right now."

"Sounds like a good plan."

We head up the pitted unraked beach to the house.

Even with the daily rake there is still a bump and a dip where I made a sandcastle last week. It was no ordinary sandcastle. That day a JCB had showed up in the carpark, a whopping big digger on tracks.

I'm good at hydraulics and somehow, I don't know how, I persuaded the Gypsies, to let me have a go. We waited until the beach was nearly empty then I drove it to the beach edge and started. I had quite an audience. I dug a deep moat, deep enough to fill itself and piled the to create the tallest castle ever.

By the time I finished with the machine there were about twenty people watching. We all jumped in the moat, all the gypsy kids and some tourists and shaped the massive pile of sand in the middle. It was impressive.

Despite endless people jumping on it, it survived a few days, then one night, on the full moon, unbelievably the tide came right up the beach and softened it into the bumps here now. No one thought to take a photo of it. Next day the JCB was gone.

The Med is full of surprises, virtually no tide then in one night it comes twenty feet up the beach, next day just how it was.

There is a rustle in the dry leaves in the trees as a warm wind picks up. It's sustained and gathers strength, whipping up sand and dust. It disturbs the surface of the sea, causing great arcs shimmering in the moonlight.

The bamboo roof up at the café is whistling as the wind passes through. It's strange, otherworldly, not something we've experienced before. Then, with one last whoosh, it's gone. The trees return to silence.

"That was strange," I comment. "Really weird, maybe the weather is going to change."

"Naa, that's not going to happen, this is the south of France, not Brighton."

As we walk up the slope to the carpark we can see the house in all its glory. A couple of people are retrieving parasols that had been lifted clear across the carpark by the wind. What a place, I still can't believe it.

I think most people's idea of a perfect house in the South of France is quite different, maybe lots of rooms and a pool to laze around and do nothing. Not me, at least not now, not now we've created this.

Yes, it's only made of rendered breeze block, yes, it's only power comes from a single extension lead, and yes it has no inside running water, and only two bare rooms, but to me? To me it's a mansion, a palace even. I came skint with a tent and now have this, and tonight it's quite a sight. It's an achievement greater than any other in my life so far.

There must be about twenty people now, some sitting around our long table made of two café trestle tables end to end with various part broken trestle benches and a bunch of old café chairs, some metal and plastic.

To start with we only had four chairs, and there were six of us, not to mention a growing number of visitors. So we had a rule, if you came more than twice you had to bring your own chair.

One by one they started to appear. Some of them probably lifted from skips, but others clearly have come directly from café terraces. You can recognise them, the green and yellow ones for example come from the Brit Camp, and the red ones from the Charlemange. We didn't really care as long as we had something to sit on.

The chairs and table live on the concrete slab that runs in front of the house we like to call our patio. At one end Jerry has his camper parked, side door open and two speakers hung on the side playing directly from the camper stereo our only source of music, and always the risk of a flat battery.

Those not sitting are dancing by the van. Rappers Delight is playing, it's gone back to one of Jerry's mix tapes. We've all got mix tapes and it's a constant struggle to get them played, turn you back for a moment and 'One Love' becomes 'Young at Heart', not so great.

Most of the faces I recognise but there are always a couple of strangers in there, sometimes tourists that have just wandered in and can't believe their luck. After a week in the over lit, noisy and brash Nat camp, this place can be a real antidote. We make a few extra francs selling them beer. Much cheaper than in the bars, but of course much more expensive than we buy them from just up the road.

If you double up what you spend you are still a third the price of a regular bar. Of course, us lot, the workers, the movers and shakers know to bring our own where ever we go, and sell what we don't drink.

Making money has become a bit of an obsession. In this place if you aren't earning it you are spending it. The whole place is designed to take your money. Temptation to spend is everywhere, food drink, clothes, beach stuff. The main road is lined with shops and bars all vying to take your hard-earned cash.

We, or at least some of us decided to turn this on its head and have become the earners rather than the spenders. The victors not the victims. Any chance we get we will do what we can to become richer rather than poorer.

A day where I end up with more money than I started with is better than one then when I have less. I'm driven by Jerry. Among our group and pretty much on the whole beach Jerry is the most successful at this. Just below Jerry is me, always just below, every day the same. But that's not a bad place to be.

Some days he'll take two hundred francs, and I'll only take a hundred and sixty, but compared to most beach workers that's not unimpressive, the average earning seeming to be about thirty. Thirty is enough to live on, but really? Three quid a day? When they seem to be working as hard as we do. But it's not what you do but how you do it.

I often think that without Jerry to drive me I may have been one of those people and I have him to thank for that even though it's eternally frustrating. To beat him is a daily challenge and I pull out all the stops, but never quite make it. He is always the first of us to hit the beach catching the first flush of tourists as they lay out their towels.

Sometimes he does this by trickery, like yesterday. Jerry's big idea over our morning coffee and doughnut, 'Let's all go for a swim before work. Ok I was thinking, at least this puts us on a level playing field. To Jerry's powers of persuasion, we all agree this is a good idea and head down to the beach towels in hand.

As I wade in I turn to find Jerry, this being his big idea, is nowhere to be seen. He's doubled back, picked up is doughnut tray and ice box and is already heading down the beach. How did he do that?

It's doubly frustrating as I see him make his first big sale only twenty feet from the carpark. Bastard has done it again. After a very quick dip, leaving the others in there, who don't seem to have noticed or don't care, I'm out of there and chasing Jerry's footprints. Of course, what really matters is who gets to the English beach first.

The top earner on the beach is an Irish guy Patrick. He just sells canned drinks. He sits at the top of the English beach with his extra-large cool box and has a constant queue we are all envious of. He's a quiet guy, very cagey about what he earns, but you only have to watch him for twenty minutes to see how much he is taking. Where does he get his drinks? From the supermarket only a hundred yards from the beach. He trebles up just carrying his box from there to the beach.

Anyone could do it, but he does it best. He has a deal with the supermarket and they have an old buzzing fridge out back just for him. When he's out or running low he just makes that short trip and he's back in business again, drinks as cold as you like. Hat's off to him.

Next come Baz and Jules, still way above Jerry and me. Great people and good friends. Their product? Tea and biscuits. Genius. They do such a good job of it. They carry a large flask of boiling water and make fresh tea in a china pot, served in china cups right there on the beach. With a choice of McVities digestives or Rich Tea biscuits.

The way they tell it the china came first, then the idea. Baz, in a drunken opportune moment relieved a terrace café of them. A bus boy had been diligently collecting them and left them in a plastic tray, similar to the ones we sell our doughnuts from, on a table close to the road, and in a fleeting moment it was gone. Baz had it. Cups, pots, teaspoons, the lot.

They make about four hundred Francs a day between them hopping from group to group always busy They make a big deal about it being proper real English PG tips and provide a moment of familiar comfort to every kind of English holiday maker.

As we approach, I can see them arriving from behind the house carrying their own box of beers, of course. Jules is twirling a café Kroonenberg parasol over her shoulder, maybe another gift for our camp?

"Did you feel that wind?" Baz calls out. "I nearly lost my hat."

"Crazy, eh?" I reply.

"I think it's a Mistral, or the beginning of one."

"Mistral?" I've never heard the term.

"It can pick up towards the end of summer, sometimes it goes on for weeks. Ultimately, it's the Mistral that spells the end of the season, not any lack of sun."

"Really?" How had I not heard of this?

"It whips up the sand and moves it across the beach in waves, like the Sahara, and it gets everywhere, in your eyes, in your mouth, you can't sit in it for long."

I look up at the sky, crystal clear and sharp as ever. "Well, whatever it was, it seems to have gone now."

"Don't you believe it." Baz laughs.

Baz and Jules always welcome at our camp, and they bring biscuits. There are several 'workers' camps dotted around the edges of town, apparently all tourist towns have them, some just a couple of tents others have grown into small communities.

It's best to keep them small, under the radar no more than four of five tents on patches of scrubland or under trees for shade. And of course, there are the official workers camps, for the legit workers at the campsites and bars. These are always in the worst places, saving the best spots for the paying campers, but they can be fun to visit, although not all welcome us, there's a bit of a thing between some of the official workers and us off the cards types. I guess they just lump as all in together.

We are the cream of a motley crew, there are a lot of good people in there, but motley is a good word to describe them. Unpredictable and often guarded, most of them live on their wits year-round as a matter of survival. Many travel a well-trod route of seasonal work, usually picking or gathering harvests.

From tulip bulbs in Holland, to grapes in the south of France, right down to the clementine harvest in

Spain. For them, this is their summer holiday. Yes, it's tough work, but compared to most it's a doddle, and the money is better.

They are used to living on next to nothing spending what they have on food and shelter, but here they get to have some fun, feel flush even. They come from all over Europe and the UK, Scotland, Wales, Ireland, England, each with their own story.

For some it's all a big adventure, they don't really have to but enjoy the freedom of lifestyle, but for many, most, it's a question of avoiding homelessness, being on the streets back in the UK, they have slipped through the net, some of them drinkers or drug users, others just can't get a break through no fault of their own, they are the forgotten and they've come across the channel to try their luck.

They make me realise that no matter how I think 'I don't fit', I've been lucky really, bottom line, I've always had a roof.

We used to do the rounds of the camps when we were just camping ourselves, always out visiting, but now with the patio and music and the table people just tend to come here. It's where it's at and the only camp right on the beach.

We know where most people live, but not Baz and Jules, it's a mystery. They disappear at the end of the night and nobody knows where. I can't blame them, none of us use banks, it's all cash and can build up. Once someone knows everybody knows, but now nobody knows, so it's ok.

A cash stash is an important place. Absolutely nobody knows where mine is. I used to keep it buried outside and this never felt good, now I'm inside behind lock and key it's safer but not entirely.

Amongst the strangers that visit us you never know who the scallies are, and at nighttime the door always wide open. Mine is within the walls of the house, literally. I won't tell you exactly where and challenge you to find it.

One night I had the idea to work away around one of the breeze blocks with a knife, like Escape From Alcatraz, until it came free. I remove it when I need to and keep my cash in the hollow centre, then slide it back in and it's almost impossible to tell. I never do this unless completely alone, usually at the end of day. I like to put money in and hate to take it out.

I'm not a money head, I never have been, mainly as I've never had any. What my stash represents to me is safety, safety from who knows what, hunger mainly. There are plenty of transients that don't eat well, this is a tough place and it's easy to go under, all too easy. Some people, many, arrive with nothing, I mean absolutely nothing, just the clothes they are wearing.

It's hard to get your toe in, that's why some start off begging. This is enough for some but it's just basic survival. Others see opportunity, maybe not to get rich, but at least to achieve a lifestyle they are comfortable with.

A tent, sleeping bag, a few cups and plates and something to cook on, that does it. This was my mindset when I arrived. As long as I can survive, I'm doing ok. But beyond survival came into view, success even.

I'm not rich by most people's standards, I imagine most would look down on me, but to me, right now, I'm living like a king, me and Jerry, kings of the beach. It didn't come overnight, but here we are, still here and doing ok. Better than ok, I've got a house! I'm the only person I know that sleeps within four walls and it feels good.

"Hey Baz, Jules, how you doing?" I call out. "Good day?" Always the first question.

"Not bad," comes the reply. "A bit hot, wasn't it? Trying to sell tea as cooling and refreshing isn't easy on a day like today."

"But you did."

"Damn right we did, just the one run though, we skipped our afternoon shift."

"Do anything good?"

They both throw their arms in the air and exclaim, "Aqualand."

"No way. I wish you'd told me."

"Would you have come?"

"Probably not, doughnuts to shift, but I like the idea."

Aqualand, what can I say? The name says it all. It's a big water park in Agde, about 10 kilometres down the road. Waterslides, wave machines. If I take a rare day off, this is a good place to go.

There is a tall perimeter fence all around, but this hasn't stopped me yet. I'm not paying for it if I can bunk in. They make enough money. I take a change of t-shirt, a different colour, in case I'm spotted. I do a quick change once in, and I'm good for the day.

Last time we used a ladder, I was with a mate, a bit of a scally and he had the idea. It was on a Sunday and there was a building site nearby, so he slipped in and came back a few minutes later with an extension ladder over his shoulder, smart move.

Up and over in a second. It's a bit far to drop for me, so it's a scramble down the chain-link fence... and away into the crowds.

That week we'd had some visitors down from London, they stayed in one of the hotel campsites down the beach. No one knew them that well, they were more friends of friends. Nice guys, but to be wary of, four of them, gangster types from Peckham. Not big-time crooks, but almost certainly not legit either. They had plenty of cash and were happy to spend it, we had a funny couple of days with them drinking in bars in town. I spent my own money though, somehow, I didn't want to be indebted to them.

On this Sunday they had decided to do Aqualand too. We travelled independently with a vague arrangement to meet up inside. It seems they had the same idea of bunking in, but not being climbers found an opening door near the ticket turn-style. It led through an office and into the park on the other side. I bumped into them very soon after, they were deep in conversation making a plan.

One of them had spotted a cash box on a table at the far end of the room. They were planning how to steel it. It was just possible it was full of cash. They asked me if I'd be a lookout. I wanted no part of this. Who were they? I left them to it and got as much space between us as I could.

Did they nick it? Yes, they did. Did they get rich? Nope, it was empty. Well, that's what they said, but they were all in a pretty good mood that night, so who knows?

Mate, that was my lot with them, they didn't see me again. Everything we do is under the radar, we don't rock any boats and although not always possible we try our best to stay out of view of the authorities. This on the other hand was high risk, high profile, and nuts.

I sit with Baz and Jules at the end of the table. Cassie sneaks a change of mix tape while jerry is not in sight. Kid Creole, Annie, I'm Not Your Daddy starts to play. Sitting around us are the Canterbury 4, Jerry and I coined that on the way down. Bill, Euan, Lizzy and Susan. They aren't actually from Canterbury, it's just where they went to university, and where we happened to meet them.

Bill I've known for a few years, since before he left for Canterbury, he's a genuinely nice guy, quiet, clever, generally happy and easy to be around, the others we just met at the party. Looking at them now, amongst all this I wonder how they might have got on had we not ventured down to their party, not so long ago, although it also seems like years.

Without us, the camper and our spirit of adventure they never would have found this place, they would probably have stayed on Gerard's crappy farm on the first night. I reckon they might have stuck it out for a week or so, bouncing around in the back of a van, but probably not much longer.

That first job seems so far away now, like a dream, a bad dream. We know a couple of Gerard sellers; they are most definitely the lucky ones being on our beach. Gerard's best, for what that's worth. I hear they are making about eighty francs a day.

Most make next to nothing, not even enough to live on, plenty just pack up disillusioned and go home. The braver ones stay on to find their own path. Probably, including us, most of the people here started with Gerard or Richard before thinking sod this, there must be an easier way.

It turns out Gerard and Richard, bitter rivals, vying for the same customers with the same products on the same beaches, are brothers. That is one dysfunctional family. I found this out one night while chatting to be what turned out to be their third brother. He told me they all use to work as a team, they had the whole place sewn up, no competition so they could sell what they liked and creamed it.

They were making good money but didn't get on and were always fighting, actual fists apparently. So, they went their own ways. They had 2 vans with the family name LaCote but split and changed their signage to their first names. Now if they were to meet it would result in an all-out brawl.

He went on to tell me they make a lot less money now, even though the beaches are busier and laid the blame on 'unlicenced' beach sellers. I kept quiet, pretending to be a tourist, this was fascinating.

Of course, the real reason they do worse now is their product. Their doughnuts are pretty much inedible blobs of gloop. Sometimes I'll buy one just to joke about it and hold up in comparison to ours. No competition. This really pisses their sellers off, so I try not to do it in front of them, but a laugh is a laugh, and laughs get sales.

"Hey Bill, how you doing?" I ask. He's caught the sun today, especially on one side; he must have dosed off in it, easily done. You've gotta oil up before heading out, the sun can be brutal, especially on a day like today.

"Not bad, not bad," he replies, emptying his stubbie. "I don't suppose you've got any beers?"

I hate it when people ask me this; beers are profit, I can't just give them all away. "You know I'll have to sell you one, I have to make my money back."

"That's OK, do me a price?"

"Go on then." Even at mates rates, I'm still doubling up. There is absolutely no reason he or any of them couldn't do the same, but they prefer the easy life and that's fine by me, just as long as they don't complain about it.

There in is the fundamental difference between the Canterburyians and me and Jerry. We are hungry for it, it's like a big game of real life. Being skint is stressful, being hungry even more so, so my stash creates a buffer between me and that. Life can still be stressful but that's not one I have to worry about for now.

I get up to retrieve a fresh box of stubbies I've left in the Gipsy's chest freezer. It's actually luck I remembered as otherwise they would have all popped overnight. As it was they are going to be perfect, freezing cold, but not actually frozen. I put two boxes in earlier, forward thinking. I take them both out but only carry one back.

Placing the box on the table I peel back the lid and write in magic marker '3 for 10 francs'. That's about 30p each. They cost about 12p, 100 yards down the lane. 'Anyone else want one? Mates rates all round', one case only.' Woosh, they are gone. Nice, I'll wait a bit before retrieving the other one.

Not a bad night.

"I've brought you this," Jules says, twirling her parasol in the air. She puts it through the hole in our old café table. "It was in a skip. I can't see anything wrong with it, just one of the wires was a bit bent and I straightened it out."

"Thanks, nice one. Can't you use it yourselves?"

"Naa, we're fine."

There was that mystery again.

The music comes off for a second and comes back on with Smooth operator, that'll be Bill's tape. Jerry looks disappointed, he was cranking it up to party, but for now it's a bit more mellow. I'm happy with that, I'd prefer to chat than dance.

It looks so great here tonight, mostly because of the new lighting, a string of 40watt white light bulbs. Alex brought it over yesterday, again, he got it from a skip. He knows what he's doing around electricity, and by making it a bit shorter he fixed it. He lives in a van and doesn't have power, so he gave it to us. He's here most nights anyway.

We've got it strung from the house to the corner

of the camper. It lights up the whole patio. Thank you Alex. He's fixed up my electrics too. When I moved in I only had power through one extension lead coming through the window, which of course wouldn't close and lock. So Alex made a hole through the wall and ran a wire through from the lean to at the back and now I have indoor power. We don't need much, just lights really.

This lot, us here now pretty much represent the best of the beach, 'the cream of the bums' someone once called us, we were never sure if that was a complement. Something sets us apart from the rest. We all work on the beach, we have similar jobs, but some do so much better than others. You get out what you put in. All in your hands, no one else's, it's on you.

It seems most of the lower earners, about 80%, see work as a drag, something they'd prefer not to be doing. You can't blame them; it's hot, the boxes are heavy, you walk and walk in the full sun while others are lying around having fun, and get little reward.

On the face of it, it's tough, just about bearable. It's like a trap they are stuck in and can't seem to break free. It's not that they are not giving it their all, they are, just not properly thought it through. I often wonder if I would have been in there had it not been for Jerry setting my targets so high.

Looking around the table here, we've made it our own. Tough as it can be, it's not a task, it's more of a game. Just how well can you do? And how? Fine-tuning it as you go.

Opposite me a Clair and Ruth, 'the Chi Chi girls. They've got it down. Chi Chi are spicy sugar coated nuts. They are the other snack sold on the beach.

Like doughnut sellers there are plenty, so competition is high. They started by working for a firm, like us, and had a crappy greasy product to try and sell, and they thought, what the hell, we should do this ourselves. They spent their last frank on a big pan, ingredients and paper bags, and from recipe made their own.

They've turned it into a Tiki thing. They wear grass skirts and garlands, and one of them plays a drum, so you hear them coming. And they sing their 'Fresh homemade Chi Chi Tiki Chi Chi' song.

Everyone loves them. People wait for them, or walk down the beach looking for them, like in search of the buffet car on a train. When they stop they get a queue. They can re-stock three times in a day.

Next to them are Clive and Sarah. They sell jewellery they make themselves. A bit older than most of us they are a couple of hippies that have been doing this for years. Everyone looks up to them, they are well respected. And they know a lot, when you are in a survival world you need to know as much as you can. Things like 'Where exactly do you stand when you get arrested?'. And what should you do?

They walk the beach with a large black fabric covered board with their earrings, necklaces, bracelets and broches pinned to it. They move from group to group. They are so happy and disarming that most people invite them over. They do a good trade, they don't talk about it but you can see their board getting emptier as the day goes on. I think some days they beat us all.

Then Eric et Sylvie, the only French people here. They come from Montpellier not far from here. They have a Chariot, all licenced and legal, probably the most legal on the beach. They spend the summer in a caravan tucked in some woods just up the lane. But it's dark there and they like to keep a low profile, so they spend a lot of time here. They are cool, and bring lots of nice food with them, they are not poor.

A Chariot is an ice cream trolly on wheels with parasol above. Because of the wheels they can carry a massive box for drinks and ice creams and keep it cold. Many people, especially the French trust Chariots as the only legitimate sellers on the beach and will wait for them to come along. Typically, they will walk 200 yards and stop and a queue will form, when it's exhausted another 200 yards and start again. It's a golden goose.

Jerry and I came up with the idea of being larger than life legitimate. We invented our own uniform, white shorts, white shirt, matching straw hats. And for the doughnuts a big bright orange plastic bakers' tray with matching hand painted sign 'Mmmm! Fresh Doughnuts – Beignets Frais', and red cool boxes with white lids.

That's just where it starts with us. We've got the look, clean smart and presentable. The rest is banter, banter and attitude.

The braver you are the more you take. It's like a show. Be there, be loud and be proud. Eyes everywhere, never miss a trick, never miss a sale. If you can make people laugh, they are more likely to call you over, maybe not right away but on a future pass by.

Jerry and I work the English beach exclusively apart from our multicultural multilingual march down here and back so most of our banter is in English and aimed squarely at our market of 18 30's there for fun and a good time.

It takes about half an hour to walk it uninterrupted, so we'll probably do the sweep of the beach three times in a day. Up, down, up, down, up, down and then back home. So six passes of any one spot.

On a really good day with lots of early sales we'll take a risk and head back for a second load. A risk because it takes you off the English beach and you might not sell them, but if I do I can clear 200 Francs in a day, Jerry 240.

The uniform idea was a bit strange given who we are, but we realised without it you are just anyone. And to them you could be anyone. At least it looks to our customers like we have an actual job and are working professionally, and that makes a difference. People trust us, even the French.

It's a real art. Sure you are ultimately trying to sell them something, but at the same time you are genuinely brightening their holiday. It's a service. It's the moments they will remember when they get home.

That's the game. Play it just right and everyone is happy. And it's fun. You get to laugh a lot and meet some good people, but I can't stress enough we are greatly helped by our product. We really do have the best doughnuts on the beach, and we shout that out all day from the tops of our voices.

Holiday makers come in waves of two weeks, changing bi-weekly. Two weeks, that's how long I've got with each group to get to know them and become their favourite seller, even though they didn't know there was such a thing before they got here. Any which way, they have to know who I am and stand out amongst all the other sellers on the beach. Jerry and I have developed plenty of techniques to keep us fresh in their minds.

Along the table is Archie, he's a great guy, very funny, always offering and ready to help anyone out. There's nothing I wouldn't do for that guy should he ask, but he doesn't, he's got life all under control. I met him on my first week when I was still getting my head around it. He gave me a great motivational talk on how the system works and how to make the most of it.

He lives in a treehouse in a small patch of woodland about a kilometre inland. It's an amazing place made entirely from old pallets and scrap for the multitude of skips to be found at the backs of premises out of view from the tourists. He knows the landowner and so, as long as he keeps a low profile, he's safe to live there.

He comes down every year and every time expands his home a bit. It started as a simple box in the fork of a tree, he now has a living room, bedroom and kitchen, and inventive loo where the poo drops out of the tree house straight into a pre-dug hole under. He comes to work on his bicycle with a large top-box on the front. He's quite a sight on the beach.

He dresses like a French onion seller, with beret and striped shirt, but instead of onions around his neck he has drinks can logos. He's cut disks of the logos from drinks cans, folded the edges so they are not sharp, then by making a couple of holes in the top has them in strings, like onions, round his neck and all over his bike, it looks eye catching, which is what it's all about.

Like most of us he works the English beach, but he pretends to be French when calling out his wares. He fooled me when we first met, we chatted in French for ten minutes before he let me in and broke into English in his strong Brummie accent. He's half French on his mum's side and has spent a lot of time here, that's how he pulls it off.

Last week at the height of selling time Archie helped a guy to medical assistance that had been badly stung by a jelly fish all over his feet. The guy could hardly walk so Archie ended up picking him up and carrying him half a mile up the beach. No easy task in the soft hot sand. The guy was easily his own weight.

Jellyfish can be a problem, not often, but when they get you, it hurts like hell. I still have a tentacle scar on my right leg from a sting last week. It doesn't hurt any more, but you can still clearly see it. If you see them, it's best to leave well alone.

Recently I watched a macho holiday maker, thinking he was doing everyone a favour, spike one that had lapped up on to the sand with a long stick. He then carried it proudly across the beach in front of him to dispose of, but didn't think it through as he carried it, it dripped slime and tentacles onto the sand that he walked right through, by the time he'd got to the bins he'd been stung to hell all over the underside of his feet.

That was his holiday ended. I hear he's still got them in bandage and is just hanging around with his feet in the air as it's too painful to walk. You often hear people say, if you get stung, piss on it, or get someone else to. Gross, no thanks, insult to injury.

I hear a motorbike entering the carpark, a deep low single cylinder pup pup puping away. It has to be Dave and Jase. Yep, there they are. They first showed up a few weeks ago on this incredible bike. At first we all assumed they were rich kids, who else would have a bike like that? But as we got to know them we soon realised that wasn't the case. Both from Milton Keynes, Dave confessed how they actually came across it.

They were in Switzerland and Jase walked into a Honda bike showroom looking his smartest. He pretended to be a genuine customer, he knows a lot about bikes so the salesman was fooled. After examining and sitting on various models he chose this one and asked if he could start it, just to hear the engine. The salesman obliged and handed him the keys.

After a couple of vrooms, and looking suitably impressed, he clicked it into gear, and Vroooom, he was gone, straight out of the showroom and away, leaving the salesman standing there like a lemon. They changed the plates and are now on a crazy trip around Europe until they came across this place on their way down to Spain, and got sucked in.

There are scallies and scallies. Those who steal from individuals, or those that would miss it, are looked down upon and shunned by all, but hey stealing from a Swiss superbike showroom was acceptable, funny even. They can afford it, and it's surely all insured.

They are generally good people, although I'm a bit more wary of Jase, as he doesn't seem to have risk limits. They have a ton of funny travel stories, scrapes they've got themselves into. They have both been travelling for over a year, sometimes together sometimes alone.

Dave was recently telling me a story about a guy they'd met travelling alone who had a VW camper. They befriended him, who wouldn't? and offered to split his petrol. He was up for it, glad of the company. Then one night in a small town near Montpellier they went into a restaurant for food and when they'd finished eating Jase has gone 'Let's do a runner'. In a flash Dave and Jase, more used to this kind of thing were on their feet and running for the door.

Their camper driving friend wasn't so quick to catch on but eventually ran for the door, then realised he's left his van keys on the table. He avoided being grabbed by the waiter as he ran back in for them, but the camper had most definitely been identified.

They got in their van and shot off down dark roads lights off to evade capture and got a good few kilometres before finding a place near a beach to park. They didn't realise how far local networks travel and while on the beach came back to find the camper on bricks, all four wheels stollen. After staring in disbelief for a moment, Dave and Jae's reaction was, 'Oh well, nice to have known you, and grabbing their bags were off, after all a camper with no wheels is no use to anyone.

I could have hated them for this, the poor guy was just left high and dry, but somehow the way he told it had us in stiches. Normal rules just don't apply here. Its dog eat dog until you find a bunch you can actually trust, like the good folk here. Funny enough Perhaps I shouldn't, but I do completely trust Dave. I take this opportunity to break open my second beer box and sell them a couple.

I look up to the café on the hill and see the lights are still on. This is unusual in the evening; they must be having a gathering of some sort. I have a bit of unfinished business with Felix, he thinks I owe him 50 francs, and I don't. I actually don't, it was a miscalculation on the count a couple of days ago and I need to talk it through with him. I'll take this opportunity to pop up and see what's occurring. Miscalculations are common and there's usually a bit of haggling over the count each day, both trying to swing it in our favour.

On this particular occasion it's about drinks, he's assumed without counting I'd taken 20 cans out, but I hadn't. Drinks are heavy and to carry them all the way down to the English beach is a tough call before starting work proper.

Bit by bit Jerry and I have taken less drinks out in the morning, preferring to buy them ourselves at the English supermarket just off the English beach. We triple up on every sale and so not only do we not have to carry them so far we make more on every sale.

The Gypsies have started to notice this and aren't happy with it, but it's really about the doughnuts, and we are the best and they don't want to lose us. It's time we had this one out for good, no more drinks, just doughnuts, at least for me and Jerry.

When we started on this beach, we also took out ice creams, with a block of dry ice to keep them frozen, but it never did, and the wastage was high, so we soon gave that up. With it went the dry ice, a big shame for us as it's great stuff to have in your box to keep your drinks cool, and if you want to make them look really cool, even if sometimes they aren't, then add a splash of water to your box, and next time you open the lid a woosh of icy mist does the trick. I've sold out with that trick. You can see them drinking it thinking, hmm it's not that cold, but the power of suggestion overrides this, and they like to think they are the clever ones.

We trade dry ice on the beach, it's like a currency, I'll swap doughnuts or drinks for it. The biggest holders are the chariots. They need it, they've got big boxes and stuff that needs to stay fully frozen. But one of them might, out of kindness or for a trade, break you off a bit, it might be the size of an apple, from a bigger block that is nearly burned out.

A block this size will last all day, but not to the next. It's a waste to take it back, so whatever is not needed is tradable.

"Hey, do you want some dry ice?"

"How much?"

"Coke?"

"Go on then."

Everyone's happy. That person might split it again. So might I. Even an ice cube-sized lump will do the frosty steam in the icebox trick, and make a little difference to the actual temperature.

I'm still in uniform, gotta change, if only to keep it clean for the morning. I head to my room. The house, as we have it is made of two rooms with adjoining doorway in the middle of the dividing centre wall.

The front door opens into the communal room. We all use this space for anything we want to keep inside and for if the weather isn't great, or we just want to hang out indoors. There is no table but we sometimes bring one in from outside. There are a couple of old armchairs, but we rarely use them. My room is through that door.

I'm the only one who sleeps here, all the rest have tents, and Jerry his camper. I swung it and bagsd it. When I moved in it was cluttered and filthy. I cleaned my room all out myself, I didn't want help as it may have given them a claim. I've been in here about six weeks now and it's starting to fully feel my own.

Pretty much everything in here has been discarded by someone else. All good stuff but not up to public standards. I'm friends with some workers at The Nat Camp, a big English hotel style campsite on our beach. Tent, bedding everything already set up, just move in. As soon as anything gets slightly broken or damaged it's thrown into one of many skips tucked behind bamboo fencing.

My friends, who throw it there, keep an eye out for me. Most of it comes from there. My bed and mattress, chairs, table, a kind of camping wardrobe, bedding even, brand new quilt and pillow set with packaging damaged so they picked it out for me, in return they get my friendship, and free doughnuts. They don't take the micky with this, but I like to be generous because they really have done me a good turn and still have their eyes open.

Mate this is luxury. I am by far the most comfortable of anyone here. More comfortable than most holiday makers. It's not a villa but it has four walls, so cooler in the day and stays warmer by night. I keep it down as I don't want to give anyone the idea of challenging me for it, or even the idea of sleeping in the other room. Very few see in here.

I generally keep the door closed but the window

opens out onto the patio and is often open. It has a glass window and metal shutters. When these are closed it's more or less a total blackout in here.

Changed and feeling better for it. Doc martins, Levi 501's black t-shirt. No other shirt needed on a night like tonight but still nice to be wearing long trousers.

The lights are still on in the café, and I can see some people walking up the slope toward it. Out of inquisitiveness, I head across the car park. I bump into Susan, one of the Canterbury four, as I walk. It seems she's had the same idea.

"What do you reckon they are up to?" she asks.

"Only one way to find out."

As we walk up the slope, we see Felix on his feet and his wife Annette greeting their guests.

It dawns on us this may be a private thing we aren't invited to. I go to turn but am spotted and they welcome us in. There are about twenty in all, mostly Gypsy. We sit at the back so as not to intrude but in no time have drinks and food placed in front of us. This felt welcoming, whatever it is it's ok to be here.

Alain walks past with a guitar. What the hell, grumpy old Alain plays guitar? A few claps as he walks through the people and sits on a high stall and tunes up. I can hear our music from the patio but its only quiet and mixed with various others.

Chatting and the sounds of happy people mingling stop abruptly with the first chord. All turn to Alain. He played it so powerfully that it rings in the air. Then to my amazement, he starts playing what sounds to me like flamenco guitar.

He is a master. Big round of applause, and in his next song he sings. Oh my goodness did I misjudge that man. Annette comes over and whispers to us that these are Catalan Gipsy folk songs sung in the Catalan language. I feel privileged to be here.

It seems the reason there are so many Gypsies in this area in France is that Franco didn't like them down in Spain, so to avoid persecution they migrated north to France. It seems France doesn't like them much either, they get a lot of pressure from the authorities who would like nothing better than for this family to move on and give up this bit of prime beach. This pressure comes in the form of bureaucracy, licences to trade etc, and by actual intimidation from the police.

They are very much a culture on their own, they are a people with a shared history, language, and identity. This isolation must stem partly from the French not willing to understand them. For my part I have found them warm welcoming and caring people. And tolerant, I mean look at us, we aren't licensed to camp there but there we are in direct contravention to the law that made them close their campsite and re-purpose it as a carpark.

It was a fingers up to the authorities. Like saying 'What are you going to do about it?' Sadly of course in the long term they are playing a losing game. The authorities will eventually win.

Tonight, we are getting a small taste of what it must have been like when the campsite was open. They often tell us of these days, not so long ago.

It must have been so nice. It sounds like it was the best campsite in town. No rows of hotel style tents, a genuine campsite where people brought their own. A friendly family place where people came back year after year. Some of these people are probably here tonight.

Bernat has set up a wooden pallet next to Alain and laid a board across it. What was this? A stage? Alain's wife Sussanne joins him stamping out dances in perfect time with the guitar. Of my god this couldn't be nicer. Probably the best show I have ever seen, and it seems to mean so much to the people here.

We've lucked out on this one. Like earlier I'm thinking should I go and get the others? But no, we have been welcomed in and that's probably enough. I've never spent any one-to-one time with Susan, so all the better.

Susan has just graduated. Her plans to become a librarian made me laugh when I heard them, I mean sure it's a noble profession, but I would have thought the opposite qualifications for her present job.

Quiet calm and collected will normally earn you nothing, but somehow it seems to work for Susan, she's made it her own. She doesn't do great but not bad either, one of the few that sit between the high earners and the survivors, I believe she's on about 80 Francs a day. Of course, she has the good doughnuts too, so has a head start on most.

I heard she was the only voice of dissent when it came to me and Jerry joining them. The idea of taking a couple of South London wide boys, her words not mine, was a bit startling, to this day she finds us a bit much, but without us she'd most definitely be home in Surry by now.

Of course I'm king of the beach here, but fully aware that in real life, in normal society, she will do very well and live a comfortable life, and I will probably sign on when I get back or look for a crappy job. For now, I'm living life for the moment, and moments don't get much better than this.

In real life, back home, I could be seen by most as a looser. I don't have a single qualification, not even a CSE let alone a degree. Many of my school friends tried no harder but breezed it through exams, stayed on to sixth form and on to university, but education just didn't suit me.

I didn't like school, and school didn't like me much either. I used my wits to survive but that's about all I managed. I know I'm clever, in a situation like this I'm cleverer than most. My teachers knew it, the good ones did and were as frustrated as me when it came to showing this in my work.

My head now, as then, here there and everywhere. Here that's a good thing, back home, and at school, it doesn't seem to be. I remember the day they gave us our National Insurance numbers in the school hall. I asked one of my teachers what this was for, and he told me 'It's so you can sign on when you leave'. He wasn't joking, that really was the only path he saw open to me.

Not being able to spell, or write in any easy readable format has always been a big disadvantage. Whenever I handed a piece of work in it came back covered in red ink corrections, sometimes more red ink than my original black. It was soul destroying at times. None of them seemed to read the content but just focused on my spelling and crappy handwriting.

In the third year, I must have been about 14 we did a piece in history about the Neolithic. I've always been fascinated by this period and pulled out all the stops. I researched using encyclopaedias and school text books, I even went to the School library, a first for me, and wrote what to that day was my best and longest bit of work. I was really proud of it.

I put some ideas in there that others didn't seem to have thought of, it was my turn around moment. I handed it in… and got it back two days later. 2/10 covered in red ink and the words SPELLING, PUNTUATION, GRAMMER in massive letters right over my work. 2 out of bloody 10.

I'd put the work in, I had done my very best, in something that genuinely interested me, I'd checked it and double checked it, and I got 2 out of 10. No attempt by the teacher to actually read the content, just spelling, punctuation and grammar.

A big moment of realisation. This place is messed up. I asked my friend Victor what he'd got, it turns out 8 out of 10, and he tells me he did it in a hurry last night, just copied out big chunks from the textbook, clearly they didn't read that one either, but it was neat and tidy and he had his spelling down, so he got the marks. Never again did I try so hard, that was it for me. If my best wasn't good enough, then screw em.

My only regret? Turning up in the first place.

I've always had the feeling, 'This world isn't for me' I'm, a square peg in a round hole. But here? This is more like it, my head always being in several places at any given time is positively a good thing. It's about spotting opportunity, and imagination is key.

Here, would you believe, and I still have trouble, I'm seen as the clever one, sharp witted and a go to when people need help or advice.

This place is me... that place isn't. Maybe it will be now when I take my newfound experience and confidence back with me.

More drinks arrive at our table, a couple of stubby beers and a small glass of Eau De Vie, and free. It's not unknown but rare. The Gypsies need to make the bulk of their year's money in the short holiday season, and so like us are not ones to miss a trick, but tonight this has been turned on its head.

I can see food being taken to tables and low and behold a tray is placed in front of us. Cheeses, saucisson, a big bowl of fried sardines and of course the ubiquitous fries, a couple of large trays. Hot salty and delicious. I get my wallet out, not sure if I should offer to pay and am rebuked. OK then back in my pocket it goes.

We hear laughter behind us and turn to see four Gypsy women, about our age walking up the slope. Daughters, sisters, cousins, it's impossible to know. They are by far and away the most beautiful women I have ever met, dark skinned with a Gypsy almost Asian look about them, as all the Gypsies around here.

Last week they were sitting at a café table as I walked past trying to look cool. They smiled at me and while casually smiling back I walked, crack, right into one of the upright metal poles holding the bamboo roof up. It didn't go unnoticed by Alain and Felix who both gave me a disapproving look as if to say, 'Don't even think about it'. The ultimate humiliation.

I have tried to talk to them before, but we share little common language, theirs being mostly Catalan. I know they do speak a Little French; I've heard them talking to customers, but with a heavy accent it's hard to get passed. They smile as they pass and one of them pretends to walk into a pole to mock me, they laugh, as do I and hold my head in my hands, shame on me.

Susan asks me if I saw the plane fly by earlier. I had. Everyday a small plane or two flies the length of the beach towing a banner behind. It's usually advertising, something like 'Aqualand or Intermarche, but todays said in massive letters 'Will you marry me?' We were all talking and laughing about it. Did she say yes? What if she said no, how funny that would be.

Apparently, she did, say no that is. Susan just happened to be there as it flew past and the guy went down on one knee with is ring. Not only did she say no but was really pissed off about it and stormed off the beach. Hilarious.

To my surprise Felix joins us at our table. I think he's letting everyone know he knows me and I can be trusted. It's noticed, until then I think it was assumed we had wandered up off the beach.

Much of our communication is unspoken, through gestures. I speak pretty good French, but the Catalan accent makes it trickier, and he doesn't understand my French much either.

He gestures towards his son Alain, clearly proud, and makes an enquiring face as if to say, "You didn't expect that, did you?" I make the appropriate "yes, I'm amazed" face, then put both hands on my heart to show how happy and proud I am to be here. He understands, and we sit quietly and listen to the music. It's a moment with Felix, and I am proud.

The song finishes and there are calls for Felix. Oh my goodness is Felix going to perform? I simply couldn't believe this. It would be so out of Character. He's an important man around here, the longer we stay the more we notice it.

If you were ever to mention knowing him to a Gypsy, they insist you sent him their best regards. I have to write it down, I'm never going to remember names, but I have to remember, or it will get back that I didn't. It's clear he holds a position of responsibility.

I don't think they fear him, he's not like a godfather, its more out of trust for his status and his good judgement. He's slow-moving, generally seated with his bottle of frozen water, and contemplative would be a good word for him. Always weighing things up, thinking things through and speaking only when necessary.

To my amazement and delight he succumbs to the pressure and with a big smile stands to his feet. Smile? Felix? That's a first. Maybe a wry grin. He has many subtle faces but smiling isn't one of them. He raises his hands to say 'OK you've got me' and there's clapping and a cheer. What? What could he possibly be about to do? Again, Annette comes over to try and explain what's going on. I make all the right faces, but don't understand a word of it, we're still in the dark.

His smile now fully gone, with serious face stands beside his son on guitar and turns to the audience. Silence, background noises are filtered out by the moment. A few thwack thwacks on the guitar strings, and he takes a breath. It's like a slow flamenco, every word sung out with conviction. Sussanne accompanies with feet taps on the board.

We have no idea what he's singing about, but its powerful. You can tell he would have been a master at this in his younger days but it's still powerful and heartfelt all the way. I'm, and everyone is, transfixed as the verses go on and build as they do.

Then for a chorus, on an invisible cue all the Gypsies in the audience, that's most of them join in, some standing, and sing together in harmony and impeccable timing, like a choir in a strange language. Goosebumps. What is this?

They all know every word to perfection; without rehearsal it seems to come straight from the heart. I see Annette singing, and a tear run down her face. This brings a tear to my eye and I notice Susan is the same. Music has never had this effect on me before and we have no idea what they are singing.

I'm trying to hold back tears. The song ends. Again silence, no cheers, just handshakes and thanks as

Felix goes to sit down. What just happened? Alain and Sussanne start up again, it's still amazing but Felix was surely the star of the show.

After spending virtually no time together since we got here, Susan and I just shared what might be the highlight of the whole time. I will never forget this. I clear my throat. 'Wow, that was something' 'I'm speechless' Susan replies. I'm thinking, 'well no change there then'.

This, this is what the authorities are hustling out. This must surely be the most beautiful thing happening on the beach for miles in either direction. The only genuine, not for pure profit happening anywhere in town.

This feels real, to all the fakery surrounding us. Out there everyone is always pleased to see you, but it's your wallet they are interested in. You hear it so much 'I'm so glad you came. Here I've saved your favourite spot. How are you today?... followed by 'Is there anything I can get you'. It translates as, 'give me your money'.

It must be getting late now; it's been dark for hours. I never wear a watch, I pride myself on being able to guess the time sometimes to the minute, but I can get it wrong, especially if there is alcohol involved. I'm clueless and cheat by looking at Susan's watch, It's nearly midnight. We are no longer alone at our table; enough people have arrived to fill every seat. Food and drinks still flowing.

Several empty bottles and shot glasses in front of me, I have the idea of clearing some tables for them. I do this in the early evening sometimes after the count; it usually earns me a cold beer or two. As I try to stand, I realize this isn't a good idea. I narrowly avoid falling backwards over the bench but am steadied by Susan. I'm clearly drunk, who wouldn't be? Those shot glasses of the homemade must be 90% proof.

"Maybe it's time we left?" I suggest.

"Yep, good call, let's leave them to it, it's their night really."

We wave a few goodbyes and I stumble and trip while walking down the slope, I'm more drunk than I thought, much more. I can see our place has thinned out, there's only Jerry, Baz and Jules and the other Canterbury three. It looks nice, still lit up by the new lights. I won't stop long, I need my bed.

My god, what happened last night? I don't even remember coming in here. How did I get out of my clothes? Aghh, what the hell is happening in my head? I feel like I've been hit with an iron bar. Am

I going to be sick? Don't be sick, don't be sick, I keep saying to myself. Ouch, ow ow ow. It's nearly pitch black in here, and I'm looking for something to be sick in, just in case. My god, this is the worst hangover ever.

There is a tap on my door. 'Hello? You OK?' It's Lizzy's voice. 'I've made some coffee, do you want some?. She opens the door a crack and the light makes my eyes hurt and my head hurt even more. 'We were worried about you, are you ok?' 'Yeah yeah, I've felt better'. 'Coffee is here if you want some.' I'll be there in a bit.'

She leaves the door open just a crack for some light. I can hear voices in the other room, that's a bit unusual. OK I'm pretty sure I'm not going to be sick now, but slowly does it. I pull on some clothes and try and take some steps to the door but trip and tumble head over heels over my trombone case. How many times will I do that?

I love that trombone, that's why I brought it, but it doesn't get used as much as I thought it would. It's just so loud I never really get the privacy to practice, and I have to face it, I'm not that good yet, I've not had it long. Mostly I just play along to Reggae vinyl when I'm home, I do it every night until my lip gives up.

I played a bit of trombone in school, but lessons of

any kind and me have never really got on, and so it didn't stick. Recently though we have discovered a band in London called Dave Bittelli's Onward Internationals. We know them as 'The Onwards', they play World and Latin music excellently, an incredible band, of amazing musicians guaranteed to get absolutely everybody dancing with mostly instrumentals.

We see them wherever they play. On trombone is Annie Whitehead, a fantastic player and she in no small way inspired me to rethink trombone. A few months ago I had a motor bike crash and having already fixed the forks by the time the insurance money arrived I had £100 to spend. I got a King 2B trombone. I pick up courage to tell Annie about my purchase and she has offered me some free lessons, but I haven't had the chance to take her up on them yet as I'm here now.

Most of the time it lives in its case. Having said that we had a very funny night out with it last week walking the though the crowds in the town centre making lots of noise accompanied by a couple of homemade drums. We optimistically called it busking, but no one gave us any money, apart from one bar owner who gave us ten francs to move on.

I lie on the floor for in the darkness a moment trying to work out which way is up. Luckily no damage done. There is a sound in the air I don't recognise, what is that a plane? but it's a continuous noise. Squinting in the half light of the next room I can see the Canterbury 4 sitting around in their sleeping bags. Huh? 'Here's your coffee' Lizzy passes it. I take a sip, it's just right and just what I need.

I'm confused. "What's going on here? What time is it? Has Jerry beat me on the bloody beach again?"

"Don't worry, no work today."

"What do you mean no work?"

"Because of the weather? The storm?"

"What storm?"

"After you crashed, it was unreal. The wind picked up and boom, the skies opened. I can't believe you missed it."

"I was out for the count. How did I even get to bed?"

"You whited out. Face flat on the table. Baz and Jules carried you in here. You came round but were pretty gone."

"What was that I was drinking?"

"Then the storm kicked off. We thought our tents were going to take off, I've never seen rain like it. That's why we took shelter in here. Apparently, it's chaos in town, tents blown down, people lost their roofs. There's stuff everywhere."

"Is it still raining?"

"Take a look."

Still in gentle slow motion, I open the front door. Immediately, I can feel the wind pushing against me, and water sprays in. Rain is coming down in buckets. It's brown out there, the sky, the sand, everything. We are used to seeing bright blue skies and sea, and bright yellow sand. That's all we've had since we've been here. And now this. With my head in the state it's in, it feels like a bad dream.

"So no one on the beach?"

"What do you think?"

"Yes, of course there isn't, just trying to get my head around it, what's left of my head. Are your tents ok?"

"They stood up, but everything is soaked."

A bright flash through the window followed quickly by a loud rumble tells us this isn't over yet. I finish my coffee and go back to my room. I open the shutters and close the windows firmly. I need the loo and it's pissing down out there.

I've got a coat here somewhere. I nearly sold it last week as I haven't used it since I've been here, but no one wanted it for the same reason. Its value has just gone up. At least to me it has.

All geared up in boots and coat I stand by the front

door. 'Wish me luck, I may be gone for some time'. I exit, closing the door quickly behind me and head through the wind and rain to our flush loo. It's the only one left standing and operational from a row that used to serve the campsite. Without it we never would have stayed.

I'm not paying too much attention to the scene around me, I'm just trying to get to that loo. It's only when I leave it I see the full devastation. There are chairs, bits of old wood and general debris covering the carpark.

I can see up at the café the bamboo roof has mostly gone and hanging on by a thread. Alain is trying to hold it from blowing away. With my head still pounding I go up to help. As I walk the slope the wind hits me full on and the rain blurs my vision. I lean on into it.

Alain has one end of an open roll of bamboo, the other end is flapping about in the wind. I struggle to grab it until eventually we have it under control and stash it under his caravan, which has also lost it's bamboo surround.

Looking down the beach in the direction of town it becomes clear just how bad the storm got. Debris everywhere, tents, signage, about 20 yards down, a small boat is lying on its side half submerged in the sand.

And the sea looks angry. I've never seen it like this. A deep dark rumble as crashing white waves rumble way up the beach with signs that at one point it must have reached the top. It's usual array of blues and turquois replace by brown, nearly black sharp waves with white crests. Even with the rain pouring down I can taste the salt in the air.

Alain is in shock. He tells me they thought their caravan might blow away in the night and they took shelter in the lorry cafe. He says it was much worse than this last night and can't understand why I didn't know that. It seems I'm the only person in Marsellian that didn't. The combination of the drink and the four walls made me oblivious.

I help secure chairs and retrieve a roll of bamboo from the beach and head back to the house. Rain heavier than ever, this place is on it's head. I never in a million years would have imagined this for today.

Back inside. Warm, almost steamy in here, I can hear the rain beating down on the terracotta roof tiles. People still hanging around in sleeping bags. Kettle whistles. Coffee, more coffee needed. Doh, no doughnuts.

I change into dry clothes take my coffee to my bed and try and close my eyes, maybe I can sleep this off. The noise of the rain above is stronger and it's not exactly helping. Then quiet.

Eh? The rain has stopped. Abruptly, like turning

off a shower. it didn't seem to slow down first, on, then off.

I resign myself to being up and can hear movement in the other room. Lizzy puts her head in. "Rain has stopped, we're going into town, to see what it's like. You coming?"

"Why not? Just give me a second."

I grab my 'float' money from its cup; I won't be needing that on the beach today, and we are bound to stop somewhere for something. Outside, the others are waiting. Jerry has emerged from his camper and is game. He's gutted to lose a day's money, and he had a new joke he was going to try today. They will have to wait.

As I lock the house behind me, "Beach, or lane?" Lane is agreed. The quickest way to town, we normally walk along the beach as it's nicer, but we want to see the damage. The sky is still dark, but in the distant horizon to the west is a band of deep blue sky, the kind we are used to. Let's hope it's coming this way.

A five-minute walk along what is normally a dusty track is turning into more like 20. It's mostly flooded. There are high points we can jump between, but most have got wet feet by now. My Doc's seem to be keeping it out. Should have taken the beach.

We reach the end of the lane, which is the beginning of town, or the end of town for most.

From here, headed north parallel to the beach are campsites, cafés, bars, and shops. Nothing real, just stuff to provide for the tourists. The place must be completely dead any other time of year. I don't like to dwell on that, as this must surely come to an end one day.

Most of the workers, us lot, go straight on to grape picking at the end of the summer season. There are lots of vines around here and apparently work is plentiful, lots of people say it's great. You get food and wine and somewhere to sleep although the actual work can be pretty tough.

I tried it last year near Grenoble and it was murder. I went with my friend Greg, expecting all of this south of France hospitality, and had a rude awakening. Nowhere to sleep apart from a tiny tent on a patch of dust. No food provided. Had it not been for an extended family of travellers taking us under their wing we would have lasted a day.

The work was backbreaking. We were given a small sickle, apparently quicker than secateurs, so you cup the bunch with one hand and cut it with the other. Hands black with juice and mud. The travellers had to constantly jump into our row to help us catch up and keep the line straight.

On day four Greg sliced through a bunch of grapes

and straight through his hand. As they lead him away for a trip to hospital, I remember thinking 'you lucky bastard'. It was that tough it seemed the better option. After several stitches he could work no more, so we packed it in and came home, having earned just enough to do so, almost.

My big idea this year was to try and connect with a few viticulturers and using my best French try and sell myself as a tractor driver. Some of them sell their produce 'en vrack' in town so I get to meet them.

Despite my considerable tractor skills, I can reverse a figure of eight with a trailer with ease, and my two years' experience, I haven't cracked it yet. The last guy I spoke to said 'My son does that' and I thought yes of course he does, and he's probably got loads of sons. Tractor driver far and away the best job in the vines. Just drive up and down while most are bent double and when your trailer is full, drive it to the cave.

There is usually an en-vrac stall here, but today it's deserted, just a big pool of flood water where it normally stands. En-vrac is great, a real godsend. Instead of buying wine in bottles you can take your own and fill them up. It's about half the price and you can get some really good wine. Mostly red.

The stall that lives here sells Muscat, sweet white,

stronger than wine, I think it's 18?, and great straight from the chest freezer. We drink it every night, filling our empty 1 litre lemonade bottles. Not tonight by the look of it.

As we walk into town it looks like a hurricane has just passed through. Everyone fixing, banging, tying and generally clearing up. Holiday makers are starting to emerge from their campsites to survey the damage.

Bins are over, chairs are in the road, all mixed colours as they've been blown up and down from their original cafes. Signs are broken. Big pools of flood water are everywhere, as we pass our nearest minimarket it has a couple of inches of water throughout.

The sky is lightning and all the while the band of blue sky gets bigger as it moves towards us. This place wasn't designed for weather like that. Although it all looks real enough, most of it is just temporary structures made of wooden framing. They spend only as much as they have to, to be able to rake the money in.

We take a right, along one of the sandy lanes that runs between campsites down to the beach.

Our friend Arnaud has a great café there, unimaginatively named 'The Beach Bar'. We are hoping it's still standing. It is. He seems to be doing great business to his shell-shocked regulars and looks relatively unscathed.

The café is built on various levels of wooden platforms, so high enough to let any water, or exceptional high tide to flow right under.

'Hey you guys' Arnaud calls over. 'Come on in'. He clears a table for us on the decking overlooking the beach. He's upbeat, almost pumped. 'Coffee all round?' He does this sometimes. He really doesn't mind if you just have the coffee and go, but we are much more likely to stay and eat after. He leans over to talk to me. 'I heard about you last night; Baz was in earlier' 'Cheers Baz' 'Maybe you'd like a hair of the dog? I'll put some brandy in yours' 'Please don't', but I know he will, and it might help. 'And a Coke please, and do you have any aspirin?'.

I spend a lot of time here. It's just under halfway from the café to the English beach. It makes a good stop off point, especially on the way back after a good day. He's legit and his family has had this place for years, since the days when it was pretty much the only place in town.

Despite the competition he does a good trade. He lays on a good service, he's quick, his drinks are always cold and served with ice and lemon, nice touch, and the food is good, half French half English. He's open in the evenings too so sometimes we wander down for a quick bite or a beer. It's calming, looking out over the sea after a hectic day.

He brings our drinks. It worked, we are eating. No doughnut this morning so getting really hungry. Four of us go for a full English, which comes with a mountain of fries, and the others just sip their coffee. I offer to lend them money but they say no. It's easier to be flush with some cash behind you, but if you haven't got it you don't want to borrow it either, if you can't pay it back, I get that.

I'm lucky enough, or have worked enough to have a cash stash, but even I'm wary of spending it. I always do a quick calculation of how many doughnuts did I have to sell to pay for this. In this case, about eight, maybe ten with the Coke.

As we wait for our feast I hear two sharp whistles coming from Arnaud, I look over to see he's warning me he's seen a couple of policemen walking down the lane. You'd think they've got something better to do on a day like today.

The others have nothing to worry about but if it's who I think it is I'd better make myself scarce until they pass. I was arrested a few weeks back, before moving into the house. I hadn't committed any crime, at least not any they knew about, just working for the Gypsies was enough.

As part of their ongoing campaign of intimidation they turn up from time to time and hassle us. As we are not officially licenced to work on the beach, we are careful not to be spotted leaving or returning to the carpark.

On our final approach we look up top to the café to see if Felix is there to give us the sign. If the police are there, he stands right on the corner to warn us. If he is there, so are the police, so we have to wait it out at the back of the beach until they leave. Sometimes they stay, unwelcomed, for a free coffee, they never pay for anything.

On this occasion they arrived just as I was walking up the beach. I was caught red handed, in uniform tray and box in hand. They are not nice, and they do not like us. After shouting at me, in the vein hope that by being louder I will understand, and of course unbeknown to them I understand every word, they say I have to leave town. They take my name and passport number and say they will come back and check.

They've said this before but have never followed it up so I assumed this time would be the same. Thinking I'd got away with it, I carried on as normal. That night we took a trip up to the English campsites for a night out and I met Lucy. Lucy was a student studying law of all things. After a fun night together drinking and dancing followed by some romance on the beach, she wants to come down to see our place. She was welcome, but I explained the situation and that it might not be a good idea to stay. It soon got late and as she wasn't concerned, we crashed.

It turned out she should have been concerned about coming back. The following morning there is loud shouting outside my tent. Damn, the police are back. They unzip the tent and drag us both out. I'm pissed off and a bit embarrassed by the whole thing, she is in shock. I try and console her but she is shaking, in pieces as they lead us to their van.

I explain to the police she has nothing to do with this, but it falls on deaf ears. After a stop at her campsite to pick up her passport, as if that wasn't proof enough, accompanied to her tent by a policeman making sure she doesn't run off, we eventually end up in the town police station, one of the few real buildings in town and sat in a cell.

Lucy is crying throughout and telling me this will ruin her career and while I feel sorry for her and try and console, we are both starting to wonder what it was we saw in each other so few hours ago. After half an hour or so we are told we have to leave town, and they are hanging on to our passports until we can prove we are doing so.

After much pleading in impeccable French Lucy

persuades them she's only just met me, and this time they believe her and let her go, but I'm still in it. Bollocks. So I go back home, the long walk to clear on the other side of town, I collect up some things in a bag and an old broken tent from a skip half stuffed into it's unzipped bag and go back to the police station.

More shouting, 'and if we ever see you here again...' they give me back my passport and escort me on foot to the main road, where I start walking thumb out. Immediately I get a lift from a bar owner I know. He can see what's going on and has an equal dislike for the police. He takes me about half a kilometre down the road then turns to bring me home, head down.

I never saw Lucy again. I wanted to apologise, although I had warned her, but I think she may have gone home. I have to be especially careful now not to be spotted. There are thousands of people in this town, so it's not too hard but I always have a watchful eye out. Arnaud knows all this, hence the warning. I slip out back to wait it out as the police drink coffee at the counter. While the others eat at the table, I'm served mine out back, with a fizzy aspirin chaser.

The day before we left England I went to Nobbys' in Brixton for a haircut, a super short and neat flat top, then later that day I'd bleached it as white as I could get it. It's growing out now, a bit of a mop, but it makes me easily spottable. I sometimes think of cutting it off but this is me, and they aren't taking that away. It's partly why I wear a hat while working, that and the sun.

Breakfast finished eventually the police finally leave and wander back up into town. I get a cheer as I re-join the others at the table, like a returning hero. The police could have chosen any of us that day, or all of us even, but had just gone for me. I'd taken one for the team.

This place has its darker side and the police are the bane of our lives. Without them it would be paradise, but actual paradise is reserved for the rich, not the likes of us.

Just last week I got a sharp reminder of this when I bumped into Ian and Sue. I'd met them on our first week and we got on really well. They have a dog, a scruffy mongrel called Boxer and live in their camper.

I hadn't seen them for a couple of weeks when we bumped into each other right outside The Charlemagne", the biggest of the English campsites with a huge café opening onto the roadside. We decided to stop for a drink and found a table right in the middle.

After a bit of a catch up we are joined by a friend of theirs, although the mood wasn't right, and he looked nervous. Seconds later we are surrounded by plain clothed police who ask us to stand and accompany them to a nearby waiting van. They had a phrase something like 'Let's take a walk in the van'. It turned out their friend was just identifying them.

Before throwing us in the back they searched us. While searching me I heard one of them say 'Let the blond one go'. They put Ian and Sue, and their friend into the back of their van, and as it screeched off left me standing there somewhat shaken, with the dog. Wagging its tail he had no idea of what had just occurred.

I hung onto Boxer for the rest of the day until I met a couple of their friends Boxer clearly recognised and they took him off me. Phew. I had no time for a dog.

A few nights later I caught up with their friends again, still with dog and they told me they had news. Apparently, they had been arrested for selling acid, LSD. Despite searching their van the police found nothing, but their 'friend's' story was strong enough that they held them anyway.

They had arrested their friend, and having found a bunch of tabs had struck a deal with him that if he'd identify the dealer, they'd let him go. They didn't. Not only didn't they, but they'd locked him in the same cell as Ian. To our knowledge they are still there now. Bummer.

The skys are lighting and starting to break up. For the first time today we get a blast of sun and it feels good. Jerry is doubly gutted by this. It's late morning now and holiday makers are starting to fill the beach like nothing had happened. If we'd held our ground we'd have creamed it today as there wasn't a single seller on the beach. But thinking about it Felix wasn't there so I guess we'd have had no doughnuts.

A day off is a rare and good thing, and now the sun is shining this was a perfect excuse. So we decide instead to take a trip out in the camper on a beano for a change of scene.

Not far from here is a range of hills, like small mountains, one of them has a snow cap. They are tantalisingly close, but we never have the time to explore. We decide to head there. Jerry heads back for the camper and we arrange to meet him in town at the crossroads in half an hour. Time for another drink, a beer this time, hair of the dog.

The mountains are further than they look, much further but we do eventually reach them, with the same crew we came down with in the van. We are soon heading upwards, a strange feeling having spent so long on the flat. There is a knocking sound from the camper steering wheel. We noticed it on the way down and feeling concerned drove to a garage in Sete to get it looked at.

They said it was the 'boit direction' whatever that is, and that it's dangerous to drive like it. But it cost way more than we had to fix it, so we drove carefully and slowly back to Marsellian, thinking we may head off the road at any time. But we seem to have forgotten about that now, the noise is still there as we hug the tight curves of the roads, sometimes with a sheer drop to one side or the other.

We arrive at a small town and take a look around. This place is amazing, it seems to have been untouched by the tourism that has engulfed the coastline. Big old stone buildings all around we head up on foot to what seems to be a small fortress.

It's about two o'clock and is deserted, a far cry from Marsellian which by now will be thick with humanity. The only shop we see open is a cheese shop, it looks ancient, like it has never changed.

Jerry and I head inside. It stinks, I mean really strong, enough to make your eyes water.

The owner, a tiny bald man just about tall enough to see over his counter, offers me a small piece of cheese on a plate to taste. He laughs as I smell it and recoil. Ammonia. Looking closely, it's moving, covered in tiny white worm-like maggots. The owner explains this is how it comes, and that all cheeses used to be like this. Jerry tastes it on his tong but doesn't eat any, as he points out he's vegetarian.

I can't. I'm not unadventurous with food but this was a step too far. 'Mmmm', Jerry says, pretending to like it, and rubbing his tummy, but can't stop screwing his face up. We politely decline to buy any. He doesn't look surprised. Out of the shop it's good to smell the clean air.

After an hour or so wandering the medieval fortress in the now full-on heat of the day Jerry has the big idea we head further up the mountain to the snow line for a snowball fight. We try but don't make it. Petrol is low and there are no petrol stations up here, and no matter how far we drive it never seems to get any closer.

As we head back down we can smell the brakes getting hot as Jerry freewheels it, engine off to save precious petrol. It's nothing short of hair raising and a relief to be back on the long straight roads on the flat.

About ten kilometres from home disaster strikes and the front of the van drops down and limping to the side of the deserted road we grind to a halt. At first we think it must be the 'boit direction' and soon realise it's a flat tyre. Not having a spare this isn't going to be an easy fix.

The plan is for one of us, me, to hitch home and see if the Gypsies can help, their other, out of season business being a huge scrap yard near Agde. I walk about a hundred yards to be clear of the others to find a hitching spot.

With only one car every ten minutes or so, I'm thinking 'I'll be lucky', but to my amazement the second car to pass pulls over. It's an old grey 2cv, with an even older and greyer farmer driving it.

Roof down we bounce along at full speed. Every now and then the car slows down almost to a halt, then releases a big backfire that shakes the whole car and delivers an impressive cloud of black smoke from the exhaust. My driver is unperturbed, he just laughs and does a 'what can you do'? gesture, he's probably had this car from new and knows it well enough.

He drops me on the main road at the edge of

Marsellian town. It's a good kilometre walk from here without a chance of a lift. It's hot and I'm thirsty, still feeling the effects of my earlier hangover. I'm relieved to get home and head up to the café to explain our situation.

There being no sellers on the beach the place is packed, and we are at the bottom of their priority list. Fully aware of the situation I'd left the others in I persevere until Felix finally gives in and calls his nephew Bernat over. Bernat agrees to help, result.

We climb into his very smart red BMW and with a push of a button the roof opens. We tear along the road at speeds we can only dream of in the camper. First to the family scrap yard where he knows exactly where to look amongst a mountain of old wheels with tyres still on. Throwing one into the boot we head off to find the others. At this moment by blood runs cold as I realise I have no idea where they are. After driving up and down the several options of road we finally spot the van.

Jerry and Bill are pleased to see me. The round trip had taken me a couple of hours all told. The others had done what I had, and hitched. 'The rats left the sinking ship' Jerry tells me. Bernat helps change the tyre so finally we can continue our journey.

I thank Bernat and offer to buy him a drink for his

trouble. He thinks I'm joking and laughs, I'm not sure why. I guess he's looking at our clothes, and van, and the fact we live in a carpark and considers us comparatively destitute.

It's been a crazy day, nothing as expected. I've been more than a bit groggy all day which has made it feel a like a dream. In a final attempt to clear my head a shower is in order. I'm particularly proud of our shower. It's tucked round the back of the house and is essentially a palette with bamboo screening for privacy. The water comes from the outside cold tap but runs through a long length of black hosing with a re-claimed shower head from the old campsite at the end.

We 'rescued' the hose from a roadside ditch in town, It was probably going to be used for something, we just made that something, something else. It took five of us to get it home, carrying it over our shoulders like a long black snake. After a few hours in the sun the water can be almost boiling hot. The trick is to let it run a bit. The hose is long enough that it continues to heat the water as it flows. You get up to ten minutes before it runs cold. Half an hour later it's recharged. No-one has used it this evening, so it'll be a good long shower.

Showered and changed, for the first time today

I'm feeling human. Remind me never to touch that clear stuff again. I've said that before and I'll probably say it again. It's dusk, a bit cooler tonight. The sea has calmed, and stars are out but it's slightly hazy and still humid.

I plug the string lights in and join Bill at the outside table. He's writing a postcard. 'No one else around?' I ask, 'The others aren't back.' 'They're taking their time.' 'The last I saw them, all three got a lift together. They all climbed into the back of an open backed van.' 'Maybe they're dead?' 'Don't even joke about it. They've probably stopped off in town'.

Jerry joins us with a box of stubbies from the freezer. 'Beer anyone? Lucky these haven't popped. I left them in the freezer and forgot all about them'. I pull the first frosted bottle from the box and open it with my lighter. As it opens the liquid beer freezes solid in that instant. This often happens if you over cool them. As we let them warm, I grab some more from inside the house. Not so cold but Passable.

It's nice just the three of us, possibly the first time since we've been here. I put my 'one love' mix tape on, it's my best tape. Reggae throughout from all eras from Ska to Bob Marley. Just as I'm getting settled, I can see Felix on the hill calling me up.

I go, of course, only to be told there are no doughnuts tomorrow. Apparently, the bakery that makes them was flooded in the storm and they are still clearing it up. He suggests we just take drinks out, but we both know that isn't going to happen. The money is in doughnuts. So 2 days off in a row, unheard of. I return to our table with the news, Jerry isn't happy.

It's calm and it's quiet. Just the softly playing reggae mix, which has appropriately moved on to 'I can see clearly now the rain has gone', and the sound of the waves on the beach. We don't talk, just sit there, and enjoy our beers. Jerry breaks the silence. 'Anyone fancy going out? Nat Camp?'

The Nat camp, short for 'National Holidays Camp' is second only to The Charlemagne". It's a vast campsite with bars and discos catering exclusively to the English. It's right on the beach and provides us with the majority of our customers. Bill cuts in quickly, 'Not bloody likely'.

He's not keen on that place. He still hasn't forgiven me properly for an incident that happened there about a fortnight ago. It wasn't strictly speaking my fault. I'd been chatting with a couple of English women I'd recognised as customers from the beach. It was them that had recognised me first. They were really drunk and one of them asked, 'If I give you a big kiss will I get a free drink tomorrow? I tried to back off saying something like, we'd

have to see. Before I knew it, she flung her arms around me and kissed me on the mouth.

It wasn't pleasant, she smelled of sweat, alcohol and fags and I backed away. That was it, the end of it, or so I thought. But later, after I had left it turns out her boyfriend had got wind of it and was threatening to find me and kill me.

I was well gone by then, and the only description he had of me was blond, beach seller, with white shirt and straw hat. Sadly, for Bill, this fitted him too. Him and a couple of his mates jumped Bill as he headed home. It was quick but quite brutal. He still has bruises and a possible cracked rib.

I hate violence of any kind, but there was a poetic justice in the story that drifted down the beach to us, that almost exactly the same thing happened a couple of days later, but this time he met his match, and some. He was badly hurt, and the police were called in. There were so many witnesses he was arrested and taken away, via casualty. He's not been seen since. Good riddance.

A figure walks up from the beach, it's Willy with

his metal detector, he's doing a little dance, he looks happy. He approaches us singing 'I'm in the money'. It turns out he's had a bumper day on the beach. No work for us, but plenty for Willy. The ferocity of the previous night's storm had shifted the sand and brought everything closer to the surface, making it much easier to detect. He tells us 'There's nothing like a good storm to make me happy.

He's got an old canvas ex-army bag over his shoulder and pours the contents out on the table. It's a bonanza. Mostly coins, with a few special items mixed in, a couple of rings, three gold necklaces and a couple of bracelets, one of them gold and heavy. Any of these could have been there for years, 'Help me count it?'.

We start to make piles of similar coins. He has 280 Franks all told. What with the other stuff he guesses the days catch is around 400 franks, The single best day he's had to date, and he only started when the holidaymakers started to leave the beach, so maybe three hours?

He's not finished yet, he only breezed up on his way to share a beer with us, and he's continuing down the beach. He says he's found the odd gem down that way in the past, mostly jewellery. Today it must be worth a try.

Just then the other Cantabrians arrive, looking tired and pissed off. Euan explains what had happened. Yep, they were really lucky to all get the same lift, but none of them had thought to tell the driver where they were headed, and as he drove along the main road that passes town he'd hit a couple of lucky green lights and so didn't stop.

Being in the open back they had no way of telling him this was their stop and had to watch helplessly as Marsellian Plage disappeared into the distance behind them. Their driver didn't stop again until he reached Sete. Even then it was a case of jumping from a slow-moving vehicle as it hit traffic, otherwise who knows where they might have ended up.

None of them speaking much French they'd decided to hitch back as one. Mugs. Very few people will stop for three hitchers, even two is pushing it. In all the half hour trip had taken them four hours. We are thinking, 'They should have stuck with the van, no one to blame but themselves.

Jerry is still keen to go out. I'm not that keen but agree to go to a local French bar in town that has a babyfoot, table football, table. I love babyfoot as it's known here, pronounced babi-foot. I grew up playing it having spent most summers in France, that's how I speak French without learning it at school. I played it so much it's hard to find an English person who can beat me.

The table they have in this bar is French style. Open at the top with lino pitch and cork balls painted white, as opposed to the English version with a glass top and pitch and hard plastic balls. I can play either but prefer the French style as it allows much more control and enables you to trap the ball and pass it about.

As I invariably win I like to bet on it. I've become a bit of a hustler. I'll play badly, just showing the odd bit of skill, then creep the money up with every game as I get a measure of my opponent. Then boom, double or quits, gets them every time. Usually with a bit of an audience I take them to the cleaners.

It doesn't always work, recently I got into a match with a French player, they are generally much better, he was good, but not that good so I went through the motions only to discover on the big finale he was hustling me too. We had 100 francs riding on it. It turned out to be one of the most intense games I've ever played, loud and frantic, both of us expert in passing and blocking. In the end I won by a gnat's breath on the final ball.

He was not happy; I've never seen anyone get so angry over losing a game. His ultimate humiliation being beaten by an English man, unheard of. It took all his friends to calm him down and stop threatening me.

He got even more worked up when I refused a rematch. But he was a hustler, and beaten at his own game so fair cop, and it was my time for a quick exit. They were holiday makers so will be gone by now. Time to find my next challenger.

The owner looks at me with some suspicion as Jerry and I enter. Bill has stayed behind with the others. We recently realised that English 2p coins work as a franc in some French machines including the babyfoot table. We soon ran out but asked a friend who came to visit to bring a couple of bags with him.

2p for a 10p frank, not a bad exchange rate. Mustn't overdo it though as I don't want to get banned from my local bar. He knows it's us but just can't prove it, and we spend quite a bit in here so reluctantly he turns a blind eye.

Jerry generally won't play me, I just beat him hands down 11-nil every time, it's one thing I can beat him at but it's no fun for either of us, especially as he shows no sign of improving. If anything he's getting worse. But he's happy to be my patsy to get the ball rolling, literally.

We play a couple of games, 4p well spent before

I'm challenged to a winner stays on game. Bam, bam, bam as his balls hit the back of my goal. He's a master and I'm beaten from the table. Can't win em all.

From there on there's a big crowd around it so I don't get another chance. Instead, we sit out on the terrace and watch the crowds walk by, it can be mesmeric, so many people all going somewhere, generally in the same direction. Where? Where are they all headed?

We debate whether or not Marseillian is ready for another doughnut eating competition. We did one recently on the English beach, in a 'get noticed' move. We both selected a champion from that week's newcomers, and to a big crowd set up our doughnut trays on stacked cool boxes.

It cost us in doughnuts but not much. Our doughnuts are big, one is enough, and I defy anyone to eat more than three. Jerry's champion won, although that was immaterial, he managed three and a mouthful to my champions two and a bit.

It was fun followed by a good couple of weeks, so we probably will do it again, but maybe not so much fun for the contestants. It turns out overeating doughnuts isn't good for you. They were both incapacitated for a couple of days, and it certainly took the edge off their holidays.

I offered my contestant a free doughnut when he finally re-emerged on the beach. He wasn't impressed. I gave him a Coke to try and make amends. Meanwhile throughout all his friends were waiting for his return, and buying from me. They thought it was all hilarious. For the record, my record is two, one too many.

We debate if there may be another stunt we could pull that doesn't actually have a victim. Maybe sports event? Naa, neither of us have the slightest interest in sport. Jerry suggests something musical but although he loves his music he doesn't actually play anything, and although I have my trombone I don't like to take it on the beach, the only time I tried this lots of sand got in the slide and it took forever to clean it out, it's still a bit scratchy now.

This only leaves me with my beach chair. Using my trombone mouthpiece I've invented an instrument, my beach chair trombone. I put to mouthpiece into the bottom of a tubular beach chair leg and a metal funnel, found in the carpark, on the opposite leg. It sounded pretty loud and made actual notes.

Then the brainwave to make it playable, I added a length of aluminium tent pole, put the funnel in one end and slid it over the chair leg, so I can make it longer and shorter, to make the notes change. It's fun and gets a lot of attention on the beach but I don't do it that often, it's all time out of selling.

I tend to take it out twice a fortnight to welcome the new waves of campers on their arrival days, being tuned into the flow of holiday makers is key, at least to me and Jerry it is. At the Nat Camp, where most of them come from, they are two weekers. They turn up in a fleet of white coaches. These coaches unload them, then fill up again to take the spent holiday-makers home.

It's a shame after the effort we've invested in them.

Only half the campsite changes at a time, the other half a week later, staggered. So every week we get a fresh batch, half the beach. It's like starting afresh every time. To keep our sales up we have to get to know them, and they need to get to know us. We pull out every stop to make this happen.

On their first day Jerry and I are positively competing against each other for the same people. You can spot them, white skin that hasn't even had the chance to go red, let alone tan.

The big groups are what we are looking for, that have all come down together. Couples are good and reliable but don't spend much. With a big group you can sell out in a moment. We joke with them, and tell them a few stories about the place, where the best bars and clubs are, and maybe give out the odd can as a freebie, never a doughnut.

One method I use is to trade, trinkets, gifts, for drinks with the African sellers. There are four on this beach, they walk the whole length so we may only pass each once or twice a day. I now feel I'm getting to know them, I've shared names with a couple, and sometimes will stop and talk but I know little about them.

They are I think from South Sahara. They zigzag through the hot sand from group to group, stand there for a moment showing their wares, then move on. They are polite and don't hassle, and it's surprising how much trade they do. They sell African crafts. From leather bracelets, to necklaces, to printed fabrics and long leather whips, they all seem to have these. Why the whips?

I'll trade a Coke for a bracelet, it's always a tough haggle but ends the same. I put it on, then find a big group of first-dayers, then find one of the women and take it off my wrist and put it on hers as a gift. It's not overt, I don't make a big deal of it, but it's just an extra way to keep them loyal. Above all they will remember me.

Baz and Jules have spotted us on their way to ours.

We swap to another table with more chairs. They have the news that Sue has been released, and reunited with boxer, but they've kept Ian in, with no evidence apart from one man's word.

The waiter brings out five formidables, one litre glasses of lager, German style. What the hell? It seems he's pleased to see Baz, who'd spent the day helping him fix up the café after the storm. Half of the roof had blown off the kitchen, and Baz, being a builder back home is handy with a hammer. He didn't take any money for it, so this was the landlords' way of saying thanks. I can hardly lift it. Am I ever going to finish this? Probably.

The rest of the evening takes on a familiar pattern, we are joined by some others and eventually end up on the patio. Some of us play luminous Frisbee in the car park until it's lost into the Italian campsite over the lane. We are up late, no work tomorrow, no doughnuts.

It's a crystal-clear night, no sign of the previous night's drama. The only difference to normal in that it's noticeably cooler and another layer is in order. Could this be the end of season approaching?

To those that will listen from the darkness of the carpark I do my talk on the stars and planets. How to find the North Star, I've always found this an important thing to know, where north is, but it's funny how few do, and I love to show them how easy it is. And where to find the planets, where in the sky they are likely to be, and how to spot them.

Tonight we can see Mars on the horizon, faint and reddish, Jupiter, nice and bright, and brightest of all Venus which is sitting just near the moon in all it's shining glory.

Archie is here. He's come in his mini. A great little car I've had my eye on since I first saw it. A maroon estate with wood on the back centre opening doors. Archie is a mate, and I've been out in it several times, shopping or in to Agde. He's let me drive before and knows I'm interested should he ever want to sell it. It seems he does, or is entertaining the idea.

He's got to get back to England and has a car there so has no need and selling it would pay his fare. I try and look only mildly interested, but inside I'm thinking yes, that car has got my name on it. Archie knows that too, it comes down to how much I can pay, and if he gets any better offers.

I take a quick look around it by moonlight. I'm under no illusions it's a wreck, but useable and really cool. It would be my dream to drive it back to England and restore it. My plan, because I know this will end, is to get back in time for Notting Hill Carnival which isn't far off now.

I wake in darkness; the shutters are closed. It could be any time. First thought, no work, so it doesn't matter, second thought, why am I feeling excited about something?', Yes, the car, the Mini. Archie says he's going to pop round at about mid-day and we can chat about it.

Last night I was trying to appear casual, like I wasn't sure, to keep the price down, but I'm well aware I'm not the only person with his eye on it and it won't hang around for long. Luckily for me I think Archie wants me to have it.

I spend the morning getting round to tasks that have needed doing for a while, like clearing up and sweeping off the patio. The sand builds up so quickly being just off the beach, before you know it you've got a dune, wheelbarrows full. Sand is a part of everyday life here, you can never escape it, it's in your shoes, on your clothes, in your hair, on your food. It gets everywhere.

So often a nice mouthful of food is tainted with that familiar gritty crunch. Keeping it off the doughnuts during the day is a top priority. I now wrap each of mine individually in kitchen roll, It makes them easier to handle when you've got sandy hands, which is always. Nobody wants to buy a sandy doughnut. We call them 'beignet au Sable'.

I often wonder how much sand I've eaten since I've been here, I reckon a good cup full. You take a shower and wash it all off and it feels great for just a while, just a quick trip to the beach and its back again, you can't beat it, you just live with it.

No doughnut for my breakfast so it's up to the café for saussice fritte. A treat, two spicy merguez in a length of French bread with a classic plastic carton of fritte, chips, on the side. I order small fritte, but am given large, like a family style box. And a can of Oasis orange to wash it down.

Oasis, Bali and Coke are best sellers on the beach, the Gypsies used to give us cans called 'Pchitt' and 'Sic', Honestly? Shit and Sick? Not an easy sell on an English beach, even with a bit of banter.

It's about midday and I'm keeping a close eye on the carpark. It's almost full but I've told Alain on the gate that Archie is coming and to let him through. No sign yet. I did a count of my money stash, I've got about 3000 francs, at about 10 Francs to the pound it's the most money I've ever had, by far, a small fortune. Know one knows, we all play it down, or at least I think we do, it might just be me. At home, working full time all I was living on was £34 per week. It would have taken years to save that much.

There he is. I go down to meet him. He pulls up behind Bernat's BMW. As I'm looking it over Bernat wanders over. I explain I'm thinking of buying it. He laughs. He really does think I'm joking. 'Pourquoi?', 'To drive it back to England' I explain. 'Mais pourquoi? He asks again.

He's a scrap dealer and is looking at it as such. The only value he can see in it is its weight after it's been through the crusher. He says he thinks I'm mad, but I'm not deterred.

Alain joins us next, he's a bit more pragmatic, he drives and old banger himself, although his almost certainly considerably richer than Bernat with his flashy car.

Alain appreciates the value of money and will never spend it unless he absolutely has to. Just looking at his clothes will tell you that. He gives it a good look over for me, even lies on his back in the gravel to look underneath.

He say's it's basically ok, but will need some work. I know next to nothing about cars, but I'm set on it, I'll cross those bridges when I get to them… if I get that far. Alain says I should offer 500 Francs. Archie hears this, and protests, he says he's got 2000 Francs in mind. I'm hoping I'll get it for 1000, a hundred quid. I've still gotta fix it up, although it does go, and I've got to get it back home and that's not going to be cheap.

Alain goes into haggle mode on my behalf, "Non non non, ça ne vaut pas ça." He picks at the grass growing from the wood on the back doors and tells me to walk away.

"OK, 1500," Archie comes back with.

I tell Alain, "It's ok, I can deal with this". I don't want him to lose it for me.

"I've got a hundred quid, 1000 Francs," I explain. "That's what I can afford, can you let it go for that?"

We both know that would be about the mark and shake on it.

"Yes, yes, yes, YES. A car, I've got a car. King… of… the… beach."

I offer to buy him a beer to seal the deal, and we head up to the café. Alain is there and seems happy enough with my deal. 'Deux Kronenbourg s'il vous plaît.' I beam. Archie tells me I can't have it until he's ready to leave in a few days, and I know he can't leave without selling it, so just have to bide my time.

Jerry can't bear not working, all those punters with money in their pockets and him not there to take it from them. He's cracked and chosen to do a drinks run as the Gypsies had suggested. I can see him from up here lugging that cool box across the sand. Not me, not today. I don't care if he beats me. This is a big day for me and I'm going to take it easy. Some leisure time is in hand.

I can't say it's an easy decision; the call of the beach is strong. It's a habit hard to break. The doughnuts keep on coming and we keep on selling them.

It's relentless, but for all its hardships, and there are many, the heat, the stinging sand, the exhaustion of carrying the weights long distances for long periods, and the ever-present chance you can be arrested any moment, it is essentially something I like to do, the best job I've had, by far. It's fun and rewarding.

Every day different, as different as you want to make it. It's about enjoying the company of the people you meet, and you get out what you put in. Jerry and I put a lot in, and it pays off. We are hot competition for each other, that's what gives us the edge. I know that he's out there now, not just selling drinks, but working on my customers with all his charm.

Although it's just essentially one long straight sandy beach, running North South, every section, depending on its adjacent campsite, or route from town, has its own character. If you hang around on the Italian beach long enough, you really do start to feel you are in Italy. I can't understand why the Italians come here, with so much of their own amazing coastline this seems a bit flat and featureless, it must be cheaper.

We know it so well now and adapt our calls depending on where we are, for example, 'cold drinks' in Italian is, 'bevande fredde', and doughnuts are 'ciambelle', although that's not worth knowing as they never buy them. On the German beaches its 'kaltes Getränk' for cold drinks and 'Berliner' for doughnuts, the one Kennedy famously got it wrong when he announced, 'Ich bin ein Berliner', 'I am a doughnut'. When it should have been 'Ich bin Berliner' ' I am a Berliner'.

The last stretch leading up to the English beach is more traditional, all mixed up, from town and carparks, lots of French, if you are trying to catch the doughnut moment it's sometimes worth drifting down off the English beach, it can really pay off. Anything goes in this section, any jokes or calls we can think of in every language we can.

I always play the underdog on the language front. I intentionally get it wrong for the comedy of it, but I like to make it seem like I'm trying very hard to get it right. People warm to that. I'll always stop and ask people if I'm getting it right, and let them correct me, and sometimes buy something in the process. They get a laugh and some national pride, and I earn a few francs, all is well.

It's all incidental really, just something to keep us amused as we head up to where the real action is. Ninety percent of our sales are to the English. They all bring their holiday money with them, most more than they need, and so it's our job to help them relieve them of this burden.

Banta is king, and Jerry and I in constant battle to deliver the best. Every day a new tack and new calls. It's a show, anything goes, make em smile, make em laugh and make em buy doughnuts. Jerry and I will shamelessly steal each other's lines so I'll keep my best until he's out of earshot, I'm sure he does the same.

Inuendo is king, especially with the 18-30s, we have long creamy doughnuts and love to shout about it. 'Get your lips around the longest creamiest thing on the beach'. 'What's long, thick and creamy? My doughnuts.' They go on forever with endless variations.

Obscenity doesn't work for everyone; you have to gauge your audience in earshot. Families are more likely to respond to songs, like 'D d d doughnuts, d d d doughnuts, sung to the tune of La Cucaracha, or 'Our doughnut, in the middle of our street' and 'You Can't Hurry doughnuts, no you'll just have to wait.' If the lines don't quite work, all the better, they can get a bigger laugh.

As we walk, we are looking for someone to lift

their hand, like an auction, to call us over. Often if I see a big group I'll pretend I thought I saw someone's hand going up, as an intro to get to talk to them. Sometimes I'll sit with them and open my box to get to my water bottle, with the dry ice fully charged under a splash of water the burst of cold mist can be impressive, like a genie. It's a soft sell, I quickly close it, with a 'got to keep them ice cold' line.

Recently I've been playing English market trader with full on cockney accent. 'These doughnuts sell in the shops for 10 francs, I'll tell you what I'm going to do, I'm not selling them for 10, I'm not selling them for nine, I'm not even going to charge you 8, I'm going to let you have them for 6, that's right only 6 francs, I'm a fool to myself at this price.' 'Getcha lovely doughnuts, all fresh today, best on the beach.' All the while I'm thinking 'How can I use this newfound skill when I get home?'

Jerry just a small dot on the beach now, I can see him making a sale, he'll be happier now, but on his return, after my chilled and rare do-nothing day, it turns out he's been hassled by the Post Secure, a kind of beach police who had demanded to see his identity which he didn't have. They aren't in themselves too much to worry about, although they look like police, they don't seem to have much power, I've never seen them arrest anyone, but they are closely linked to the police and will call them in if they feel it necessary.

We have got good at spotting the different uniforms and can quickly disappear when we see them. Usually we'll sit with holiday makers and cover our wares with a towel until they pass. This can be a good move as the holiday makers can sometimes feel sorry for our plight and often buy something once the danger has passed.

The three main types are, the police, by far the worst and always to be avoided, then there's the Gendarms, a kind of civil police more linked to the army, mostly they concern themselves with traffic offences but have the right to arrest, and although mostly ambivalent to us there are some real bastards in there and they can cause a lot of trouble. Then the post secures, the least bad, but actually based on the beach, so they see it all. This time they have let Jerry go with a warning, for what that's worth, and the usual get out of town or else threats.

Hanging around at camp as the afternoon rolls on the carpark is starting to empty when we see a car pull in with a trailer carrying two jet skis. An opportunity too good to miss. We befriend them and invite them over for drinks.

It turns out they are a gay couple on their way down to Spain and have taken a break here, the first place on their journey they have seen the sea, with the hope of getting their jet skis in the water.

Having decided it's not possible as they can't get them close enough to the water, Jerry and I try and persuade them otherwise.

Normally, they say, they would just reverse the trailer to the water's edge and just float them off, but this isn't possible here, so we offer to get a bunch of people to help carry them across the soft sand. When they finally agree, we realise that's going to be easier said than done. There is just me and Jerry. Determined to make this happen and with luck get a go, I head up to the café in search of help.

By the time we finally reach our goal and with the help of Gypsies and a few random holiday makers the sun has lost its heat and beginning to set. The sea is glassy smooth, perfect conditions as their engines roar into action and they zoom out to sea. We watch from the beach thinking, please, please let us have a go. After a good half an hour they finally return. We don't like to ask and so are relieved when they offer. This is going to be fun.

After a quick run through the working, and some safety talk we ignore it's our turn. We have a wristband with a cord linked to the key, so if we should fall off the jet ski it would cut out and float until we can climb back on.

Vroom, wow. We are in deep water in seconds. The swimmers have now left the beach so it's all ours. Jerry, being Jerry opens his up to see just how fast it will go, and me being me attempts to race him.

The faster we go the more they lift from the water so it feels like we are flying, but at this speed the slightest wobble will throw you in as I was about to discover. While crossing Jerry's wake, I'm in, with a massive splash I'm thrown from the ski and deep underwater, so deep I have no idea which way is up. When I surface, I can see the ski just bobbing there like nothing had happened.

The owners had neglected to tell us how to get back on in deep water and after clambering about for a while I slide on from the back, just in time to see Jerry taking a dive, he's under so long I wonder if he's going to resurface. From out here we can see the sun setting in the west and a golden glow on the water, the only disturbance caused by us. This is better than I could have dreamed. You just never know what's going to happen around here.

After what seems like hours but is actually only about 20 minutes we head back to the beach. I have half a mind they might not be so happy about the way we treated their jet-skis, but far from it, they are delighted we had such a good time.

The Cantabrieans are back at camp now and in exchange for a quick go, very quick as it's getting dark, they help us manhandle the skis up to the carpark and back on to the trailer.

What a day. We wave them off as they continue their long journey. One of them gives me his number, I think he fancies me as his partner doesn't look happy about it. We both know I'm never going to use it and it's soon lost.

As night falls and our visitors increase, it's all we can talk about. Archie turns up, and I'm quick with, "You'll never guess what we did earlier." But he's distracted and has come on foot eh?, and carrying a bag.

"What have you got there?" I ask.

"Electric petrol pump, it fell off," he replies.

"Fell off what?"

"My car, stupid." I knew that's what he meant but didn't want to hear it.

"So it's broken down?"

"Until it gets a new one of these." He shows me where the plastic bit where the pipe fixes on has snapped. He's tried gluing it, but that was never going to work.

"Can you fix it?" I ask.

"Possibly not. It's a Mini, you see, and they don't have many out here." He says he's tried phoning a few places but has come up blank.

I'm not keen to buy a broken-down car. It may be a mess, but it has to be drivable, or it's scrap metal, as Bernat had seen it. I start to think, if it's not working, it might be in my favour. Nobody is going to want a car that doesn't work and can't be fixed.

"You're probably not going to want to buy it now, are you?" he asks.

"Probably not," I reply. But it dawns on me that if anyone has got an electric petrol pump for an old Mini, the Gypsies will have. It's a gamble. If I fix it before buying it, then it'll cost more, but if I buy it on the off chance, I could be taking a big risk. But at the very least, I'd get its scrap value. I do know the scrappers, after all.

I offer, "Not working, I'll give you 400 francs, forty quid."

He looks gutted and comes back with, "500?"

"You've got a deal. Where is it?"

"Just at the end of the lane. It's got no petrol either; it all pissed out on the road. That's how I noticed it."

"Can you leave the pump with me?" I ask.

"For sure. Have you got a plan?"

"Not yet, but I might think of something."

The rest of the night is pretty typical, I sell three cases of cold stubbies, which has made up a bit for the day off.

Next morning first thing, before the doughnuts arrive I pop up to see Alain. We drink a coffee together and I show him the contents of my bag. 'It's an electric fuel pump' I tell him. He looks at me as if I'm stating the bleeding obvious, he knows exactly what it is. 'Do you have one?' I enquire He nods to say 'yes', but there's a hint of 'probably' about it. 'Can I leave it with you?' He takes it and says he'll let me know. 'When?' I ask, 'When I know' he says'. I just have to leave it at that.

Felix has arrived down at the house with doughnuts and Jerry is already filling his basket. I have to go. By the time I start to fill my tray, wrapping each doughnut Jerry is already on the beach, he's done it again.

It's not such a great day, it's sunny, but there's that wind again, not as big as before but Baz was right, it's whipping the sand up into little whirlwinds and it's getting everywhere, trying it's hardest to get into my doughnuts.

There are not so many on the beach, the nationality campsite beaches are almost empty, and even though the brits are a bit hardier our beach is half empty and they are not buying. I return with half a tray of unsold stock, unheard of.

The next few days bring more of the same and has led to a build-up of doughnuts. Felix wants to freeze them, but we discover this makes them heavy and gloopy and we refuse to sell them. This causes a bit of a stir but ultimately, we've got a reputation and don't want to lose it, even if there is no one on the beach.

I've brought the car and with some help have pushed it down into the carpark, Alain says he's going to charge me for parking it, and I point out if he'd find me a petrol pump I wouldn't have to. He has an endless and heated list of reasons he hasn't got round to it yet.

Finally, frustrated by his lack of action I decide to go down to their breakers and find one myself. I know where it is from the tyre trip. I hitch and get there with no trouble at all. Hitching works pretty well around here, although it's always a bit of a risk.

A while ago when hitching into Agde I was picked up by a creepy guy who put his hand on my leg, I pushed it off and he did it again, so I told him I'd open the door wide if he did it again. He tried, so I did, I opened the door at full speed, he screeched to a halt and I jumped out. He shouted at me as he sped off but, phew he was gone.

So I arrive at the breakers thinking I've got the measure of it having seen the wheel pile, but soon realise this place is huge, vast, it goes on for miles, piles and piles of cars rusting in the salt air. It takes me fifteen minutes to find somebody. I recognise him from the café as does he me. I tell him what I'm looking for and say Alain has sent me, not strictly speaking true.

He knows where we might find one and having walked about a kilometre through Streets of junked cars, there is a mini. From the front it looks smarter than mine, but the back end is completely stoved in. He climbs under with some tools and a few minutes later comes out with 'pompe électrique' in hand. I thank him and he says I can pay Alain.

He wanders off leaving me to find my own way back through the maze. On arrival at the carpark, I show it to Alain. He's not too impressed with me going behind his back, but it's a job he doesn't have to do so lets it ride. He does however think I'm taking the piss asking him to help me fit it, but he does begrudgingly. I forget to offer to pay, and he never asks so it's a freebie.

Jerry drops me at a garage to fill a plastic petrol tank, it'll be enough to get it going, if it starts that is. While we are at the garage, Jerry fills his camper up, he's calculated how much we all owe him for various trips out including this one. I owe him, he's worked out, 100 francs, a tenner, ouch, but he's timed it right and I have to pay him or walk back.

Back at camp, battery charged and petrol in this is the big moment. Alain and Bernat are there and Jerry, Baz and Jules. I turn the key and the engine turns but doesn't catch. I leave it a moment and try again, but the battery starts to tire. 'Arrêt', calls out, Bernat and gestures me to pop the bonnet. He does something, I have no idea what. 'Essayez? Try it? He calls from behind the bonnet. At first it struggles, then vroom, vroom vrooom, vroom, Yes. yes.

The weather stays fine but as Baz predicted the mistral wind never really gives up, blowing in varying degrees. One by one our friends start to leave town, headed to their next job on the vines, or back to the UK. It pains me to think it, but it's maybe getting time I should be thinking about it too. Although I never want it to, the season will eventually end.

I'm earning enough to keep my money stash stable but am not adding to it anymore, and with a few bad days it'd start to go down, this place isn't cheap. The numbers on the beach are steadily decreasing, as are our sales until soon it will reach the crunch, time to go.

I still have one more adventure, getting the car back to London and by now I'm keen to get going. It's not taxed, but having English plates this doesn't seem to matter, but I think it's a good idea to get insurance of some sort.

Easier said than done. Being English with and English car I can't get any here, and having phoned a couple of places in England, taking up half a day, they say I'd need to be there, and the car too to do it, which I'm not. Oh well, I'll just have to drive carefully.

I'll be so sad to let this place go, from nothing, absolutely nothing, I've built up to having a house, a car, savings and a newfound approach to life. I vow to come back but I don't think anything will beat the time I've just had.

My plan is to leave at about lunchtime tomorrow, and to spend the rest of today making my farewells. I'll leave the Gypsies until last and head into town with Jerry and Bill. The other Cantabrians have already left, by train, who knows how they afforded that, they didn't earn it. Jerry's plan is to follow his nose and maybe head down to Spain to chance his luck.

The trip out, from bar to café, to camping grounds is a bit of a disappointment, so many people have already left. By nightfall there is only one place left to go, Arnaud's Beach Bar. We've been putting the word out during the day and are hoping to see some faces.

It's a warm night, and as it goes on more and more faces arrive, it's a great night, I think everyone still left is here, it's like one big after show party. Music plays, drinks and occasional tears flow.

This is it. The formidable glasses are out and we're finishing with a bang. Looking around me now, at the sea, and at the people, the laughing, dancing, singing, it's hard to beat. I'm not just an onlooker, I'm a part of it, this is me and look where I am, look who I am, I belong, that's a good feeling.

Jerry comes over, looking as gutted as I am. "I guess this is it then," he says.

"I guess so," I reply. "Thanks, Jerry. I wouldn't, couldn't have done it without you."

"That goes both ways. Do you think we'll ever find another job like this?"

"Somehow I doubt it."

The excess of the night before pushes back my estimated leaving time. It's early evening before I make my way up to see the Gypsies and say my final farewell. Felix first, I push the house key into his palm as he did with me way back when.

I tell him the house is all cleared out which it is, I really did a good job in case I should ever return. He's pleased and put's it back on its overcrowded keyring.

Annette gives me a big hug and is genuinely holding back tears, we have become close and I really will miss her, if ever I was unwell or needed anything she was the one I went to.

Even Alain is sad to see me go. He's a grumpy old sod at times but we have developed an understanding. Neither of us like to back down, and we've come head-to-head at times, but I like and respect him and it's now seeming like this is mutual. We are from different worlds, and it's all I could hope for.

They all come down to the carpark to see me off, a deep orange red sun in our eyes as we walk down the slope, me for the final time. My car is stacked, full of the things I've accumulated and thought I would have to leave behind. My pride and joy being the vintage light up 'Bienvenu' 'Welcome' sign. I get in, roll down the window and start the engine. It's time.

Catching a last glance in my rear-view mirror I literally drive off into the sunset. Notting Hill Carnival, here I come.

ABOUT THE AUTHOR

Dave Andrews

Thanks so much for reading. I really hope you enjoyed it. Sorry no chapters, just how it happened. I wouldn't call it a historical document, but to the best of my memory forty years on most of it is true.

A little bit about me. I'm a trombonist with 40 years' experience on the UK live music and sound-system scene. These days I perform with, and record for various reggae artists and best known as King David Horns. In my other day job, I'm a designer and all round creative.

My life as a musician started quite suddenly with a 1984 following busking trip to a small festival called 'Glastonbury'. The previous year, in the summer of '83, I experienced this adventure which was to set me up for my life to follow. I brought back a new and positive sense of self-identity, confidence and ambition.

For musical context, and those of a certain age, this summer was set against the background of the following tunes playing out from every café bar and club in town.

1982 top releases:

It Must Be Love - Get Down on It - Dead Ringer for Love - Golden Brown - Say Hello, Wave Goodbye - Love Plus One - I Can't Go for That (No Can Do) - It Ain't What You Do (It's the Way That You Do It) - Go Wild in the Country" - Poison Arrow - Just an Illusion - Papa's Got a Brand New Pigbag - Fantastic Day - House of Fun - Mama Used to Say - Happy Talk - Driving in My Car - My Girl Lollipop (My Boy Lollipop) - Walking on Sunshine - The Message - Pass the Dutchie - Do You Really Want to Hurt Me - Just What I Always Wanted - Annie, I'm Not Your Daddy - I Don't Wanna Dance - (Sexual) Healing – Maneater - Young Guns (Go for It!) - Living on the Ceiling - Our House - You Can't Hurry Love

1983 top tunes, up releases

Our House - You Can't Hurry Love - All the Love in the World - Down Under - Buffalo Gals - Electric Avenue - Too Shy - Wham Rap! - Billie Jean - Africa - Never Gonna Give You Up - Total Eclipse of the Heart - Sweet Dreams (Are Made of This) - Let's Dance - Beat It - Every Breath You Take - Bad Boys- Buffalo Soldier - I Guess That's Why They Call It the

Blues – Gold - Red Red Wine - Karma Chameleon

Printed in Great Britain
by Amazon